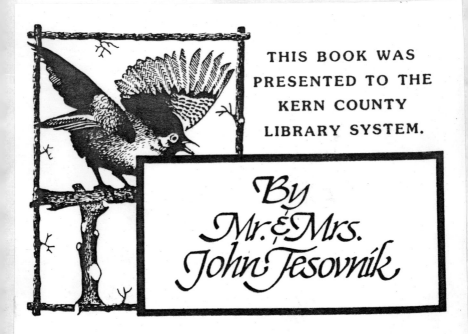

Of Music and Music-Making

BRUNO WALTER

Of Music and Music-Making

translated by
PAUL HAMBURGER

W · W · NORTON & COMPANY · INC · *New York*

Contents

CONTENTS

Introduction

This book is intended as a *finale* to *Theme and Variations*, my autobiography. Originally, I had given the latter the sub-title 'Reminiscences and Reflections', but I came to realize during my work that the book would not keep the promise held out by such a sub-title, or at most only partly keep it: the musician's reminiscences left too little room for his reflections. As a biographer, however, I felt committed, above all, to the claims of the temporal, the course of life between childhood and old age; thus it happened that the *variations*, i.e. the changeful sequence of experiences, events and new departures in my life, formed the main burden of my report, while the *theme*, my musician's self, though indirectly recognizable in the variations, had no opportunity to make itself known as announced by the sub-title through a sufficiency of thoughts and reflections that would amount to a statement of personality. But how could I have set forth the *reflections* of a musician as well as his reminiscences without overstepping the limits of an autobiography? The contents and scope of the present deliberations will answer for me—for these contain the thoughts which were actually part of the plan of my former book, but whose exposition I had to restrict considerably for the reason I have mentioned. In any case, *Theme and Variations* is not lacking in reflections and confessions that interrupt the flow of my recital; longer stretches of a contemplative nature, however, would have shifted the stress of the book unduly, and might well have destroyed its unity and construction.

INTRODUCTION

This final variation is meant to form the continuation of, and complement to, my autobiography; the continuation, in so far as my thoughts about music and music-making, resulting as they do from my life as a musician as related in the former book, have an added autobiographical meaning; the complement, since in latter years my perceptions have been somehow augmented and intensified, as is befitting to my age.

All the musical and spiritual experiences that I have harvested in the course of my activity as an executant of dramatic and symphonic music—an ever increasing and maturing wealth of observations, insights, thoughts and so on—I shall attempt to preserve here in written form, just as a careful housekeeper takes pains not to lose what he has saved. I was scarcely able to aim at formal unity, though, in a book that resulted from such gleanings and hoardings. But although the argument of this book may pursue a devious path, I hope it will reveal to the attentive reader its concentric, unified meaning. For all its multifarious contents arose from one intention; namely, to penetrate to the nature of music and music-making and to impart whatever could or should be communicated of these meditations of my old age.

The chapters devoted to conducting are, of course, meant to be of practical use to my younger colleagues and those musicians who are about to take up our profession. All the same, this part of my reflections is not intended to be a *course of instruction* in the narrower sense of the word, either—like the rest of the book, these chapters are no more than an exposition of my views, prompted by a lively wish to communicate myself. I direct myself by no means exclusively to the musician, but to all who love music and live in it, finding in it the indispensable nourishment of the soul. I wish to report, profess, even advise, but I do not presume to instruct. Indeed, to everything I am trying to tell the reader here, there could be applied the words of Wotan to Brünnhilde, 'My own counsel I seek while I speak to thee'.[1]

[1] 'Mit mir nur rat' ich, red' ich zu dir.' (*Die Walküre*, Act II).

CHAPTER I

==

Of Music

==

Thoughts on the origin of music

Two and a half millennia ago, Pythagoras proclaimed his teachings on the harmony of the spheres. To my mind, this doctrine is not just the fanciful product of a highly-strung imagination, but a true revelation granted to a sublime spirit. I firmly believe that some primordial phenomenon of nature was unveiled, in sound, to this great mentor of men, and that he, in actual fact, perceived the harmony of the spheres—though not with his physical ear. His remarkable discoveries and theories in the realm of astronomy, mathematics, and physics—we owe him, *inter alia*, a clear definition of musical intervals—vouch for the seriousness of those tenets. For everything that we know about the spirit, personality, circumstances, and teachings of Pythagoras tells us that his 'harmony of the spheres' cannot narrowly signify some exclusively physical, Babylonian-inspired interval-relation of the circling planets. After all, Pythagoras was the centre of a religious community, the proclaimer of immortality and metempsychosis, an astronomer and philosopher of rank, and we should have no doubts as to the ability of so highly inspired a man to hear with his inner ear the harmony of the spheres and to experience it as an adventure of the soul. Although no physical ear may have been able to register the flow of this primordial music, a mind of Pythagoras' organization may well be credited with the gift of receptivity for the sounding of the spheres.

Similarly, the beginning of the Prologue to Goethe's *Faust*:

> *Die Sonne tönt, nach alter Weise,*
> *In Brudersphären Wettgesang,*
> (*The sun-orb sings, in emulation,*
> *'Mid brother-spheres, his ancient round,*[1]

or Ariel's comment on the sun-rise in Part II:

> *Tönend wird für Geistesohren*
> *Schon der neue Tag geboren.*
> (*Sounding loud to spirit-hearing,*
> *See the new-born day appearing!*)

must not be narrowly understood as poetical metaphors but rather as the manifestations of an acute perspicacity towards cosmic events.

The man-in-the-street, to be sure, is inclined to dismiss such tokens of an enhanced perceptivity as rapturous illusions, instead of humbly and zealously acknowledging the clearer illumination and wider horizon of the more generously endowed mind. Yet there may be few 'plain men' who, below the starry dome, will remain totally inaccessible to a more elevated interpretation of their place in nature; I am fairly certain that the soul of any but the dullest person is moved by the nocturnal firmament in a mysterious, harmonious, yea, musical manner. It may even be that the juxtaposition of 'the starry sky above me' and 'the moral law within me' in Kant's noble dictum, goes back to the influence of Pythagorean revelation.

I have increasingly become conversant with Pythagoras' and Goethe's idea of a primordial music, not perceptible to the sensuous ear, but sounding and soaring throughout the cosmos. Tracing it to such exalted origins, I began to understand more deeply the essence of our art and its elemental power over the human soul. Man, being a creature of Nature and subject to the cosmic influences that inform all earthly beings, must needs have been under the sway of that music from his earliest days; his

[1] Transl. Bayard Taylor.

organism reverberated with its vibrations and received its rhythmic impulses. These spheric events, instinct with universal significance, and their influence on the development of man, must have determined man's musical propensities, which— from an appropriate point of sensory and spiritual maturity onward—were to blossom forth in musical utterances of living sound.

The consequence of all this would seem to be that everyone must be musical 'by nature'; and indeed, I do maintain this to a limited extent: in the sense, that is, in which everyone is able by nature to speak and to understand the spoken word. A man who took in a musical phrase as an unconnected series of sounds would be as totally unmusical as another would be wholly unintelligent who appreciated a clear, simple sentence, not according to its sense, but as a string of disconnected words. I would not deny that music might be an unintelligible noise to some. But this would be anomalous, an exception from a generally valid law, an absence or reduction of one of the faculties that go to make up the full man. On the other hand, man's elementary gift of music is as little guarantee for a specific musical talent as is his normal gift of thinking and speaking for a poetic disposition. All that I wish to point out in this context is the intrinsicality of music to the universe—which, of necessity, must have its effect on the highest species, man—or, in other words, the inner relationship between Nature and Music.

The development of music from an elemental life-force to a fine art is intimately bound up with the history of the human psyche, permitting, perhaps, a deeper insight into the unfolding of man's inward faculties than his progress in other cultural provinces. In the development of music from the above-mentioned stage of first maturity to the creation of our great works of art, the creative potentialities of man and the exalted origin of music are likewise manifested; for only man, the creative, was able to produce such results from the elemental potential of music, fashioning it, in the course of the centuries, into a powerful language of the soul; and again, only the primal, transcendental element in music can explain the decisive step forward in man's creative urge, putting him on the road on which our music lay. In contradistinction to the sculptor who shapes lifeless material into a work of art, the composer has to build his work from living, incorporeal sounds, the immanent laws of which leave their imprint on his work. Thus, the absoluteness of music is woven *into* the product of the composer's creative imagination as an extra-personal, preternatural sound, vibrating within the personal, reality-bound musical vocabulary of our great masters, and testifying to the exalted origin of music.

Musicians, too, have borne witness to this intrinsic sound-image of the universe. In Gellert's poem *Die Ehre Gottes in der Natur* ('The Glory of God in Nature'), the elemental style of Beethoven vindicates, with solemn conviction, the message of the pious poet: 'Die Himmel rühmen des Ewigen Ehre—Ihr *Schall* pflanzt seinen Namen fort' ('The heavens praise the eternal God's name—they *resound* to his glory'). A similar poetic testimony to the immanent music of the universe has kindled such imaginative response in another composer, Robert Schumann, that he felt compelled to express his agreement and enchantment in the highly inspired *Fantasia* for piano in C major. These are the strange lines of Friedrich Schlegel to which we owe the existence of Schumann's work, and which preface it as a motto:

Durch alle Töne tönet	(Through all the sounds
Im bunten Erdentraum	of this motley life-dream
Ein leiser Ton gezogen	there swings one soft note
Für den, der heimlich lauscht.	for him who listens intently.)

By 'all the sounds of the motley life-dream' the poet can only mean the sensuously perceptible sounds of human activity or manifest nature, such as the soughing of forests, the surging of the sea, bird-calls, thunder, storm, and other mundane acoustic phenomena. Amidst all this elemental turmoil, however, the 'intent listener' hears a sound from spheres beyond this earth.

From the liveliest pieces of music whose rhythm and tunes may invite the listener to dance, over the whole gamut of musical expressiveness in its limitless variegation, to the otherworldliness of a Bruckner Adagio, all creative and interpretative activities of man point to an origin of music in the spheres of the coursing stars. Our art of music, pervaded as its temporal manifestations are by its essential, timeless character, does not only exert a decisive influence on our culture but is also a message from higher regions which exhorts us to be aware of our own higher origin.

Thoughts on the essential nature of music

From my early days on, I have felt that music is more than a purely artistic concern. As a young man, I was already disinclined to see in it an art like any other. Man's gift for the *visual* arts finds models of colours and patterns in nature which through the eye work on his soul; from the wealth of visible objects rises the spark that incites the creative talent to depiction. Nothing comparable is given by Nature to the sense of hearing: whatever audible phenomena there are cannot—in a way analogous to the process in the realm of the visible— spark off the urge to their artistic representation in a talented listener. Thus—granting such exceptions as the bird-calls and thunderstorm in Beethoven's *Pastoral* Symphony—it could never happen that the physically audible should become the subject-matter of musical creation. For it is not the sensuous ear—albeit an organ closer to the soul than the eye—which perceives that 'intrinsic essence of the world' which, according to a profound philosophical definition, is demonstrated by music; it is an organ of the soul, which we can with justification call 'the *inner* ear', that receives the powerful stimulus towards musical representation which emanates from the *intrinsic* essence of creation.

It was thus borne in on me by my daily contact with and growing appreciation of our art that music is a world in its own right, removed from the other arts, and that the mighty river of our music as we see it before us, springs from, and is replenished by, a hidden source which lies outside the world of reality. Music ever spoke to me of a mysterious world beyond, which moved my heart deeply and eloquently intimated its transcendental nature.

I refer here, of course, to music in general, that is, absolute music which is nothing but itself, as well as vocal music which is influenced by the word. It may appear that the latter is an objective, representative art taking for its aim, perhaps, the descriptive rendering of the text; in actual fact, however, it is able to deploy, while doing justice to the word, its full, autonomous musical power beyond the limits of language. Shouldering, as it were, the word on its flight through its limitless domain, transmuting its meaning into a musical one, dissolving it in music, vocal composition remains, at least in the works of the great masters, true to the spirit of absolute music. The art of music, born of cosmic origin, acquired in the course of its development through the creative genius of man an intensification of its expressive powers which now embraces the most humanly personal statement; well could Schopenhauer say of music that its exclusive concern was with 'our weal and woe'. But this, in its widest sense, is a fundamental theme of every man's life. Thus, the incomparably intimate relation that exists between a sentient human being and music is explained by the fact that within the mighty universal flow of sound man recognizes the beating of his own heart.

If, for the moment, we disregard what is *expressed* by music, and turn our attention to its essential character, to the sublime order of its sounding, moving universe in which a creative spirit unmistakably reveals itself, we shall be inclined to consider music a parable of creation itself, ruled by the logos. I am of the belief that there is no more immediate access to an understanding of the logos granted to man than by way of music, which bears resounding witness to the latter's divinely creative and ruling character.

THE ESSENTIAL NATURE OF MUSIC

Yet it is not only the unmusical who might refuse to place the notion of music, its composition and interpretation, in so exalted a context. It is quite possible to be musical in the ordinary sense of the word, to love music and even exercise it with talent, and yet consider any not strictly intra-artistic view of music as high-flown. These sceptics should ask themselves, however, why it is that music has attended almost every sort of communal ceremony in the life of the nations, and in particular those solemn rites that draw our minds to the supernatural. The use of music in religious cults is well known, dating back, with the Greeks, to Homeric times. This function of music as a contribution to worship can only be explained by its transcendental nature; its consolatory impact on suffering humanity may result from the fact that the frequently meaningless and painful *text* of life (to quote Schopenhauer's bold metaphor) is rendered meaningful to the groping mind in its interpretation by the *melody*. Thus, the setting of sacred words as we find it in the musical part of divine service has always been considered a legitimate employment of music; even those who reject any but the aesthetic view of music will feel that the setting of sacred texts is natural and germane to the nature of music. The combination of music and religion has always seemed pertinent to both the religious and the aesthetic mind. The universal significance of such works as Bach's *St. Matthew Passion* and B minor *Mass*, Mozart's *Requiem*, Beethoven's *Missa Solemnis*, Handel's *Messiah*, Bruckner's *Te Deum*, etc., springs not only from admiration for their supreme artistic standards, but also from a general conviction that the essence of music is commensurate with religion.

It does not, of course, follow from this proximity to religion that music's transcendental message can only reach our soul by attaching itself to words or images of the religious sphere. On the contrary, music is immeasurably more powerful for being uncommitted, deploying, as it does, its most impressive eloquence in absolute and, above all, symphonic music. It is in the highest forms of absolute music that the workings of the logos find their clearest reflection, and can thus be symbolically grasped by us. In view of the multiformity and boundless extent of the realm of music, however, we are faced with the following questions: is transcendental significance an essential attribute of music, or does it only pertain to its highest manifestations? And how can it happen that music may descend from its lofty place, stooping to banality and vulgarity; how can one call by the same name of music what spills out from dance-halls and bars, or assaults us, with yowls and screeches, in the grotesquely distorted melodies, harmonies, and rhythms of jazz and allied forms of dance-music?

The answer would seem to be that there is no such thing as 'music in itself', and that music, having its existence only in the written works of composers, is dependent, in regard to the value and character of each work, on the talent and skill, inspiration and intention, and spiritual and ethical qualities of every composer. The character of music, as that of every other art, can be superlatively ennobled by chosen individuals, or debased beyond recognition by the inept, inferior or perverse.

And yet, as I have pointed out above, music is not mere *material*, helplessly delivered into the hands of the composer for any and every use, as is the amorphous, dead clay in the hands of a sculptor. The elements music consists of, the cells, as it were, from which musical organisms are made, have their own life; they can only be combined in compliance with the innate laws by which musical language is ruled as verbal language is by grammar. In the first place, there are the twelve notes from which the composer has to construct his piece, joining them to simultaneous and successive sounds, grouping them into patterns, and establishing time-relations between them. In their boldest as well as in their simplest combinations there are active those elemental laws, the elucidation and systematization of which are the task of the theory of music. The composer who were to sin, intentionally or unintentionally, against these fundamental laws would only produce 'non-music'.

I am strictly referring to tonal music here, for any musical consecution without a tonal centre, in an imaginary atonal field, seems a-musical to me. To every musical mind these fundamental laws have always seemed natural, that is, founded in the nature of music, and the atonal composer's revolt against them is as senseless as would be a rebellion against the laws of physics.

Familiarity with these laws immanent in the function of the elements of music was inborn to me as to every musician, and theoretical studies only went to confirm what we knew instinctively and experienced in the daily round of making music. As I have pointed out in my essay *Von den moralischen Kräften in der Musik*, what seems to me the most significant trait of that autonomy of the elements of music is the striving of the dissonance towards resolution in the consonance. A conflict demands solution, unrest yearns for rest. I think I am right in finding here an allegory for an inner law of the world; I would even submit that a sharper eye than mine might find in this elemental sequence, in this striving for peace and conciliation, the quality which enables music to be the carrier of the exalted message I mentioned before.

Seeing that every composition consists of a combination of elements in which these immanent laws reside, one should assume that even the most ordinary piece of music would evince, by virtue of the strength of those self-sufficient elemental forces, some vestiges of the altitude at which the spirit of music dwells. I have often asked myself whether this is not so; whether, that is, the heavenly drop of nectar contained in it does not give to even the most trivial musical concoction that contrasting flavour which makes it so deplorably attractive.

While the elementary laws of verbal language, which we call grammar, are of a rational kind, I recognize in those of musical language an emotional quality. The drive from movement, unrest, conflict to peace and rest, although it renews itself with every dissonance, always comes to rest eventually in the final consonance of a piece, and thus is invested with the optimistic significance of a promise. This may explain why even the most sombre piece of music does not plunge us into hopelessness. Amidst the negation of a tragic composition we perceive the positiveness of the very element in which it expresses itself; music confirms to us the insight that came to Nietzsche when, at dead of night, he looked at the world: 'Joy is deeper than grief'.

In Grillparzer's masterly story, *Der arme Spielmann*, we read of the author overhearing this most humble devotee of music as he played his violin in entranced solitude; it was a single note that he bowed again and again; swelling and fading, he delighted in sustaining it, then alternating it with the fourth, the fifth and the third—it was obvious that this simple production of notes with an occasional change gave him great happiness.

And must we not agree with the 'poor minstrel' that a mere sound of definite pitch—unlike the spoken word with its indefinite pitch—has the power to stir our feelings? Even a single note, this most humble messenger from the exalted sphere of music, contains a little of the emotional quality we find in its elements and which, heightened to a spiritual revelation in the stupendous works of the great masters, floods over us and shakes our hearts.

CHAPTER II

Of Music-Making

Myself and others—of musical interpretation

When I think back to my childhood, I well remember how by making progress on the piano I became more and more conscious of my own soul, my own ego. It was myself whom I discovered, myself whom I experienced ever more intensely in my abandoned playing. Although I opened my heart with joy, and sometimes with reverence and awe, to the music I played, it was first and foremost the pleasure in my own piano-playing that determined my relation to music during many years of my childhood. I rejoiced in being able to unleash the power of sound through hand and heart; what I played mattered only in so far as it helped me in giving expression to my own talents and emotions. I luxuriated in drawing forth with my fingers the splendour of the *forte*, the gentleness of the *piano*; I was delighted when I succeeded in investing lyrical themes with a smooth, singing *legato* tone; I revelled in the agility of my fingers, the vivacity of rhythmic propulsion. More and more, my whole being came under the spell of music-making, my temperament was kindled by it, my heart poured its warmth into it. Thus, I remember with certainty that as a child I did not try to arrive at an understanding and enjoyment of musical composition by means of my talent, but, on the contrary, employed a work of music as a vehicle for enjoying my own talent.

In the later years of childhood my relation to music underwent a gradual change; I soon realized that there was more in Mozart's C minor *Fantasy* than I could put into it. Without touching the keys, I sat in front of the C sharp minor Prelude from the *Well-tempered Clavier*, losing myself in its melancholy. The more profound the works became with which I occupied myself, the sharper became the line within myself between the finished product and my interpretation of it. The romantic ardour of Schumann's *Fantasy* for piano in C major became a source of deep enchantment; incomparably deeper, in fact, than would have been the mere satisfaction of having found a peg on which to hang my pianistic ambitions. This definite turn towards the supremacy of the work of art in my musical development was completed as I came to understand—in the years of my adolescence—the symphonic literature and the quartets of Beethoven.

From the psychological point of view, it is not so difficult to understand that stage in a young musician's development when the compositions he plays serve merely as a springboard for the testing of his own wings. He cannot have reached the musical or spiritual maturity needed for probing the depth of a work of art; he is yet lacking in the knowledge and experience that could make him appreciate it in its details, let alone in its entirety. What is more natural than that musical talent should first show itself as a delight in making music?[1] In music-making, the youthful temperament and enthusiasm of the young musician, his song-bird joy and rhythmic fire, find full vent; in music-making, the young, striving soul, sustained and uplifted by the element of music, finds its liberation from every-day life—the ego becomes aware of itself and its powers.

When, after years of slow maturing, we have come to understand the work of music as a revelation of creative inspiration; when the composer and his work have become the *dominating* factor in our inner life; when we have put ourselves at the *service* of this 'other one' and his work—will the voice of our soul then go from our music-making? Will the delight in exer-

[1] Translator's note: the original has 'Musizierlust an sich'.

cising our own talent cease to be one of our musical impulses? Will it be replaced, perhaps, by humble submissiveness to the intentions of another? The answer is an emphatic 'no'. If a pianist, in Beethoven's E flat major concerto, wishes to put himself fully at the service of Beethoven's genius in his rendering of this dithyrambic work, this does not imply an act of servile self-negation. On the contrary, he will only be successful in his endeavour if he freely unfolds his own self, to the limits of its capacity. In bringing to life the fire, the grace, the melancholy, the passion of the composer's work, what can he call upon but his own fire, his own grace, melancholy and passion? The more notable a person the interpreter is, the more powerful will be his interpretation. The insignificant interpreter will drag a significant composition down to his own lukewarm sphere; his weakness will dim its beauty and conceal its depth; his confusion will trouble its clarity. Greatness is needed for understanding and expressing greatness; tenderness and passion must be his who would perceive and represent another's tenderness and passion; none but a fiery apostle can promulgate the fire of the prophet. In short—as I have pointed out before, in my essay on Gustav Mahler—it is only the great reproductive artist who is able to penetrate and proclaim the work of a great creative artist.

Thus, the ideal musical interpreter will be one who is wholly taken up with the work, wholly in line with it, but who, at the same time, conjures up the full force of his personality—and this includes, of necessity, his delight in his own talent for interpretation. He will have preserved the joy in music-making of his young days, and he will be right in pouring his innermost being into his interpretation since it has undergone a union with that of the composer. Yet though I may fully understand Beethoven's *Hammerklavier* Sonata, having appreciated its musical meaning, its form, and the emotional depth of each single feature, it does not follow from this that I can play it now in Beethoven's style, giving full due to its Promethean stature. Our incessant struggle with the countless details may have taken us towards Beethoven time and again; we may have become at home in the sphere of this particular work—every great work of art is a world in itself—yet all this amounts to no more than the pre-conditions of an authentic interpretation.

For the act of musical interpretation is accomplished in two stages of opposite tendencies: the first is a 'taking-in', the second a 'giving-out'. The success of the second stage depends on that of the first, but by no means follows from it. Between the two, there is a partial 'change of level'. Each requires a different order of mental qualities, and success in our task depends on the right equilibrium of the various sets of forces involved. We often meet musicians in whom the power of assimilation is more highly developed than that of execution, and it makes us sorry to see that a person of deep understanding may yet fail in the reproduction of a work of art. How often does it not happen that a composer is a feeble interpreter of his own work—which surely must be utterly familiar to him. The converse disparity between assimilation and execution exists, too, though perhaps less frequently. Sometimes, many of the virtues characteristic of the good performer, such as fire, colourfulness, energy, a flair for lyricism and brilliance, the communicative drive of an interesting personality, are found united in an interpreter who is either unable, or not seriously trying, to penetrate to the true meaning of a work of art. This is the type of the virtuoso who, following his natural bent, is much more concerned with a fascinating execution than with revealing the work to us; the work will remain in the shadow cast by his glittering personality.

But how, in the ideal case of our internal forces being balanced, does execution arise from empathy? How is the largely spiritual, gradually evolving first stage—the assimilation of the work—converted into the dynamic, time-bound, second stage, the execution? Now, there is such a thing as reproductive inspiration, which compresses the entire, multifarious results of a prolonged study of a work of music by which one approaches a composer, into *one* spontaneous outpouring. This form of inspiration re-creates, in the specifically interpretative talent to which it is bound, the particular sphere in which the erstwhile *creative* inspiration had taken place. In this way is born what we may well call an authentic performance. It is only when the creative impulse which has engendered a composition reverberates in every detail of a performance, that we can speak of an authentic interpretation.

Let us now glance at the different, yet related realm of drama —related, since here, too, a work of art, handed down to us in notation, is to acquire the life-like reality intended by its author through a re-creative effort. The actor who, by a study of Shakespeare's drama, has become fully conversant with the character, the problems, the sufferings, the fate of Hamlet; who masters the verses he has to speak, and feels an affinity with the character, or at least the salient characteristics, of his hero, is still not fully equipped to represent Shakespeare's Hamlet on the stage. In the case of the actor, too, all this is no more than the foundation from which the spark of reproductive inspiration must rise. By its agency, the sum of all these insights will coalesce to a total vision of Hamlet, to a clear, perceptional image, into which the actor may step, thereby virtually becoming Hamlet. Looks, gait, gestures and speech will now bear the impress of this inner image into which the actor has been transformed.

In my autobiography, I mentioned the histrionic genius of Mitterwurzer, who was a veritable Proteus.[1] By an elemental impulse of his talent he was able to transform himself, in appearance, voice, walk and gestures, into a completely different human being. His gift for metamorphosis proved itself in greatly divergent roles, such as Goethe's Mephisto, Schiller's Wallenstein, the droll figure of a Saxon theatre-director, and others. A similar talent was to be found in Albert Bassermann[2]:

[1] Translator's note: Friedrich Mitterwurzer (1844–97), Viennese actor of classical and modern character-parts (cp. Bruno Walter: *Theme and Variations*, English Edition, 1947, p. 74–75).

[2] Translator's note: Albert Bassermann (1869–1952), famous German actor of modern, and later classical, roles.

the Ulrik Brendel of Bassermann's early days was in every respect the terrifying figure of an aged and ruined man, showing traces of former greatness and power; the actor's intensely credible impersonation of this figure from Ibsen's *Rosmersholm* could, in its complete integration, only be the result of a sudden, visionary apprehension of Ibsen's figure, and the actor's consequent, spontaneous transformation into it.

The task of the actor is like that of the re-creative musician in that he, too, has to come to terms with the 'other one', the creative poet, whose imagination must be his beacon, and whose work, confined to mute print, must, by the powers of his personality, be awakened to full life in motion and speech. His task, as ours, is one of assimilation and reproduction. But the mute signs of music, the notation and the directions of the composer, allow of an incomparably higher degree of certainty for authentic reproduction than the words and directions of the dramatic poet. The latter give no indication for the change in pitch which is of such importance for giving meaning and life to the spoken word, nor, normally, for the pace of a scene, the slowing down of a word, or the speeding up of a sentence. At best, we get general directions that are open to many interpretations. How exact, by contrast, are the clues towards the meaning and expression of a phrase as given in musical notation! The unambiguous notation of pitch and of the rhythmic correlations of notes gives a clear picture of the author's intentions, and the latter's directions for tempo, dynamics and other things are like so many signposts leading us on to a faithful reproduction of his work.

The problems of the actor are seen vastly to exceed those of the re-creative musician in complexity when we consider the visible side of the actor's task. The indications of the poet's intentions, so scanty in verbal as compared with musical notation, are not only to supply him with the meaning and spirit of the words, but are to give rise in him to a life-like conception of the drama's figures, of their movements, gestures and relation to each other; yet withal, the actor's imagination must be confined within the bounds of re-creative art and his vision tied to that of the poet as it is manifested in work and word.

The comparison is not altogether valid—I am well aware of it. For the actor's efforts are directed at a *single* figure of the drama while the musician is concerned with the re-creation of an entire work. To call to life, from the written text, the *drama* in its entirety, is the job of the producer; thus, it would seem that he might be a better object for comparison with the musical executant than the actor. However, the realization of the drama by the producer remains indirect; between him and the *other* whose work he is to re-create, there stands a third person, the actor; and it is he who must transform himself into the character created by the poet, giving it life of his own life. It was, therefore, the actor—in spite of his task being more limited than the musician's—who seemed a better basis for a comparison between the two forms of reproductive art, which, despite many divergencies, are clearly related in essentials.

Whereas, from the words of the poet, figures beckon to the actor who look, speak and move as do the people of the bright, real world of the actor's experience, to us musicians there rises from the printed page the dark world of sound with its irrational shapes, a kind of Faustian 'realm of the Mothers'[1] to which we are admitted only by the magic key of musical talent. Here, we find a reality more mysterious than the man-inhabited world of the actor; and yet, we are just as at home in our world as the actor is in his. We conceive its variations, developments and involutions as life-like images into which we may bodily step, as the actor steps into the life and fate of dramatic characters. Thus, for the re-creative musician, too, a path is open— analogous to the actor's—from the assimilation of his subject to its reproduction; a path from one self to another. For we, as well, are transformed: the pianist identifies himself with Beethoven's E flat major concerto during a performance; the separation between the ego of the player and that of the *other*,

[1] Translator's note: the reference is to Goethe's *Faust*, Part II.

the composer, is abolished. The principle of individualization melts in the fire of such mystico-musical union, and nothing can be more real or experienced more securely than this mysterious act of unification between us, the work, and its creator.

'I! I'm going full tilt!' is what Dostoievsky's Dmitri Karamasov shouts in ecstasy to the driver as he speeds along to the decisive meeting of his life. And this is exactly how the re-creative musician feels at his great moment when a notable work is challenging all his powers. The great task does not make him small and modest—how could smallness and modesty convincingly proclaim mightiness? No, it is *his* ego which rises to its utmost heights. 'He! He is going full tilt!'—that means, he is in the middle of things, all is set in motion by him, he is everything, ego, work and creator, and there is no longer room for 'another person' or an 'external object' in this enhanced, transmuted ego and in what issues forth from it.

But let me add that the struggle with the meaning, style and individuality of a work cannot be successful unless there exists an affinity of character between executant and composer, smoothing the way for the former into the latter's creative sphere. Without the innate harmony of their hearts, the interpretation will sound strange, cold and unconvincing. The scherzo of Schubert's C major symphony I can only make my own if the stormy life-force of the first subject and the soaring blissfulness of the second subject strike a kindred, Schubertian note in my soul, thus evoking my spontaneous, gladly-given loyalty. The end of the funeral march in Beethoven's *Eroica* can only become my own if my heart is in sympathy with that unique tragic darkness.

I cannot, however, give any practical advice as to how one is to achieve this incorporation of foreign matter, this identification of and union between interpreter and work. It is an act of grace that occurs when a true musician humbly and intensively studies a work with which his being is in accord. I am quite aware that my description of the process sounds rather involved and might discourage a young musician. But then, so would a description of the process of walking. The knack of using his legs, on the other hand, is inborn in every healthy person; equally, the born musician is instructed by his musical instinct in the use of his talent, and is enabled to attain by a direct route his goal of establishing a union with the work of art. No other instruction would be of help to him. Nor was my exposition meant to be in any way didactic—I was merely concerned with stressing the importance of the executant's personality, and with encouraging the interpreter in the full use of his own talent in music-making, by pointing out to him the possibility of identifying himself with the work and its author; I also wanted to prevent his being overawed by an erroneous conception of the notion of 'unselfish service to the work'. I shall speak below of that other, more frequent, and insidious danger besetting the interpreter, namely that of overstating his self to the detriment of the work. Here, I merely wish to state that the interpreter cannot fulfil his task unless he takes full responsibility as the work's ambassador, and that he will fail to communicate the music strongly and convincingly, in a meaningful and feelingful performance, unless his own soul speaks from his loyalty to the work.

Of tempo

In his essay 'On Conducting'[1] Richard Wagner wrote: '. . . But a correct conception of the melos alone can give the proper tempo: the two are indivisible; one conditions the other'. And further: 'To sum up in one word the question of a tone-work's right performance, so far as depends on the conductor, it is this: Has he given throughout the proper *tempo*? For his choice and dictation of that tells us at once whether he has understood the piece or not. Upon closer acquaintance with the piece, the proper tempo will give the players almost of itself a clue to the proper rendering, whilst that tempo itself is direct evidence of the conductor's acquaintance with the latter. How far from easy it is to determine the proper tempo, however, is shown by the

[1] *Über das Dirigieren* (1869).

fact that only through a knowledge of the correct rendering, in every respect, can that proper tempo itself be found.'[1]

No musician could deny the axiomatic significance of these sentences; and, indeed, Wagner's subsequent reflections, which are supported by conclusive examples, have been widely accepted.

The next generation followed Wagner's authoritative words with such zeal that he would hardly have had occasion to reproach its music-making for those undifferentiated tempi which are the main point of censure in his essay. Unfortunately, however, as Wagner's influence spread, his teachings were perverted and exaggerated by a considerable number of musical executants who now fell into the opposite error. While the conductors against whom Wagner's philippic is directed had not grasped the necessity of modifying the tempo, so that the living substance of a work often became a prey to meaningless uniformity, it has since become necessary to take a stand against an exaggerated modification of tempo, leading to an equally meaningless restlessness and arbitrariness. The type of the Philistine, whose heart could not be moved by the living, creative inspiration of a work of art, has been succeeded by that of the virtuoso who, not content with the autonomous life of a piece of music, thinks he must enhance it by an over-differentiation of tempo and delivery. Too little was followed by too much, and I am sure we act in the spirit of Wagner's teaching if, today, we warn against excess as he, in his day, warned against deficiency.

What, then, is the mark of the *right* tempo, the finding of which is, according to Wagner, the paramount task of the conductor? It is that it permits the musical meaning and the emotional significance of a phrase to show to best effect, and that it allows for technical exactness. Seeing, however, that in the course of a piece of music its content, mood and technical requirements change incessantly, the tempo has to be adapted

[1] English translation by W. Ashton Ellis, from *Richard Wagner's Prose Works* (Vol. IV), London, 1892–99.

to this change to remain always *right*. Let us therefore state that the notion of the right tempo for a piece is relative, not unlike that of the right clothes for a journey which will depend on the weather and other circumstances. All the same, our problem remains that of *tempo*, not *tempi*. For the well-constructed piece of music in organic form—which alone concerns us here—is defined by *one* main tempo which, though it may change in the course of the composition, maintains a continuity that accords with the symphonic continuity of the composition. From this the further conclusion can be drawn that we must remain at the same speed until a change in the design of the music forces us to modify it. The right delivery, which is to be made feasible by the choice of the right tempo, demands a flexible continuity of tempo—let us call it 'apparent continuity'. So much is implied in Wagner's teaching, and it is in this direction, above all, that the trend of my own considerations moves; these are, of course, intended not only for the conductor, but for interpretative musicians of every kind.

Apart from certain pieces such as the third movement of Beethoven's piano sonata in D minor, op. 31, no. 2, or the C sharp major Prelude from the first part of Bach's *Well-tempered Clavier*—compositions, that is, whose musical meaning resides in the unbroken maintenance of a strictly even flow of semi-quavers—all music is like a river of varying degrees of fall, with the concomitant fluctuations or modifications of its speed. Those events in the course of a composition which require a noticeable change in speed, have been provided for by the composer himself in the form of directions, such as *ritardando*, *accelerando*, *più mosso*, etc. This fact alone should prove that noticeable changes in speed, other than those marked by the composer, will offend against his intentions, unless, as the case may be, a painstaking interpreter should have come to the conclusion that such a change was indicated by the meaning of the work and the implied intentions of the composer, and the latter had merely neglected or forgotten to prescribe it. This means that all other modifications of tempo, as they correspond to the ebb and flow of the music, must be of the unnoticeable kind. In other words: continuity of speed is one of the most important principles in music. The absolute validity of this principle is not diminished by the fact that the ebb and flow of the music produces what is, metronomically speaking, the above-mentioned 'apparent continuity' of tempo.

I should like to point out to the reproductive musician who permits himself unwarranted changes of tempo, as *ritardando* or *accelerando*, *meno mosso* or *più mosso*, that this implies a revaluation of the meaning of those passages that were intended by the composer to have an even tempo. For *ritardando* and *accelerando* are not merely indications of motion; they also have the emotional significance of hesitating and urging; besides, the sudden entry of a *meno mosso* or a *più mosso* has not only an emotive effect, but often also gives the impression of a formal paragraph, of a division in the course of the music. It is scarcely necessary for me to stress that we reproductive artists must not indulge in such arbitrary, disruptive acts affecting the soul, as well as the form, of a work.

Noticeable changes in speed that are not demanded by the composer are, therefore, misrepresentations; whether they result from intellectual presumption or from sheer licence, they deviate from the author's intentions, and thus from the purpose of reproductive art.

'What pedantry!' I can hear many a musician exclaim. 'Should not a performance have spontaneity and the flair of improvisation? If we stay strictly in tempo, except where the composer himself interrupts the continuity, then the restraint imposed on us by our endeavour will rob our interpretation of all immediateness. Why should I not obey my heart, if it prompts me to hold back here, to press on there, to retard one phrase and accelerate the next? My performance will sound spontaneous since I am playing the music in the way I feel it, and not as the composer compels me to play it.'

My answer to that is that the tempo directions of the composer are an integral part of the notation of the work; the changes in tempo demanded by him are part and parcel of the composition.

Ex. 1.

This passage from the fourth movement of Beethoven's Ninth symphony shows what I mean by this. The music here expresses hesitation, almost to the point of coming to a stop, until the decisiveness of *tempo I* puts an end to hesitation, and leads on to the wild resurgence of the *presto*. Played without *poco ritenuto*, *poco adagio*, *tempo I*, the music would lose the dramatic significance intended by Beethoven. These directions are, therefore, not superimposed from the outside, but belong, *from the moment of conception on*, to the *composition*, which, without them, would lose its meaning. Not to effect the changes in speed demanded by these directions would be tantamount to destroying the meaning of the passage thus marked, and depriving it of its emotional significance.

Seeing that changes of speed can have such influence on the sense of a musical phrase, we should beware of changing the speed in the absence of the composer's direction just because our personal taste or the leanings of our heart would have it so. Since directions, as those quoted from Beethoven's Ninth, are part of the composition itself, their neglect—no less than the introduction of tempo-changes where they are not prescribed by the composer—is in the nature of an encroachment on the composition as such. And where would be the limit to such encroachments? Once we deprive a phrase of the sense given to it by the author's directions, or give it a sense not asked for by him, why should we not go further, and boldly obey the bidding of our 'heart' when in some passage it wishes to change the notes and rhythms prescribed by the author?

My idea of the spontaneity and improvisatory character of a performance is quite otherwise. Certainly, we must not be under any constraint while playing music. We must feel free, but free within the laws whose binding force we have recognized when we chose to be musical interpreters. If we should chafe under the immanent laws of a work of music as under a compulsion, we are not made to be its interpreter.

For the criterion of our talent as reproductive musicians lies exactly in our capacity for assimilating the intentions of another so completely that not only are the demands made by the work no burden to us but that we feel them to be our own demands. Only thus shall we feel free within the limits of the laws imposed on the work by the author, and only thus will our music-making sound spontaneous, since we now are free to follow the bent of our own heart which has learnt to beat in unison with that of the composer.

Let me stress once more that the continuity of tempo on which I insist must contain no element of compulsion, let alone metronomical rigidity. A tempo which is always *right*, because its almost unnoticeable modifications cling to the changing content of the music, will flow forth naturally, and never sound rigid. And it is just this *natural flow* that I am driving at.

Untouched by the constraint of an unfeeling uniformity as well as by the licence of wilful change, we have to find our right speed which will enable us to perform the music in lively and natural fashion. As an example of the widespread trend

Ex. 2.

towards arbitrary tempo-changes, I should like to instance the above passage from Beethoven's *Eroica*; it is often played with such deliberate retardation, particularly in bars 10–13, that its association with the main tempo of the movement, and dependence on the latter's character, is almost entirely lost (*see* Example 2).

Richard Wagner quotes the same example, but with the contrary intention of demonstrating how it loses its meaning when it is rattled off at the main speed without any modification. I cannot but heartily agree with him when he demands for the rendering of this passage a modification of speed such as is required by the intensity of its expression and for the proper preparation of the *sforzandi*. But I feel equally certain of Wagner's approval when I demand that Beethoven's express intentions should here be realized by means of those light, hardly noticeable modifications of speed which do not disrupt the closed form of the movement, and that the distinct *ritenuto*, prevalent nowadays, which painfully upsets continuity, should be avoided.

Speaking of the Allegro of the *Freischütz* overture, Wagner says that he feels in no way trammelled by the more gentle character of the second subject, since he is self-reliant enough to take it imperceptibly slower. Imperceptible—that is the key-word for those liberties by which we keep the tempo 'right'.

Drastic, disturbing tempo-changes that dispel continuity, however, must not always be considered as sins committed by hardened sinners, as wilful interferences with, or capricious misrepresentations, of the composer's clear intentions. Often this sin is committed from pure motives; that is, from the conviction that a change of speed is the only way in which to express the deeply-felt meaning of some passage; or again from the desire to make an important detail particularly impressive. I am speaking from experience, for as a young musician I have often been culpable of such sins; yet judging by my attendant goodwill, I was not so much sinner as victim to my excessive sensitivity.

It was not an easy way that led me to the realization of the paramount importance of 'apparent continuity' in shaping a tempo. It led from my errors and miscalculations as a young conductor, through stubborn battles against my inborn bent for effusiveness, to a very gradual improvement. It took me a long time to learn enough from my mistakes to be able to correct them and attain to a purer style of making music. It was part of my nature to fall in love with every beautiful detail of a composition and try to reproduce them with all the intensity of expression of which I was capable, and thus neglect the synthesis and unity of conception which are the main point of an authentic interpretation. My enthusiasm for details was stronger than my capacity for subsuming them under a higher order.

Thus, in my early music-making, one kind of expression would follow another, one climax hand on to the next, without strict planning or subordination to the form of the entire work. My interpretations suffered, therefore, from a sort of softness, or even weakness, of which I became painfully conscious in the course of time, without being able to do anything about it. The turn to the better was made when I discovered, at last, that what was missing in my performances was the regard for the work in its entirety, without which its greatness, seriousness and unity will not reveal itself. It became clear to me that it was the emotional extravagance of my immature heart that had made me neglect this main aspect of a piece, and thereby the symphonic style; helpless against my emotional compulsion to express all and everything, I had done damage to musical form. I gained firm ground, at last, when I realized that here is a method of interpretation higher, nobler, more in accord with the greatness of the work, than is indulgence in the sway of one's feelings: the method, namely, of directing one's attention to the entire design of the work, its structure, its general emotional content, and never losing sight of these through the intensive cultivation of details. I recognized then that the most indispensable and surest means of attaining this aim is to shape the tempo as a well-fitting dress is shaped to clothe a healthy body; only thus will the organic form of a work of art become manifest, while interruptions in, or arbitrary deviations from, continuity will, like so many unruly creases, prevent the clear recognition of that form. But it took time to advance from this inner realization to a practical victory over my old habits and to a mastering of that higher method; it was relatively late that I succeeded in modelling my musical efforts on those moral and spiritual ones of a family father who knows how to reconcile the justified wishes of each child with the well-being and harmony of the family as a whole. He knows as well as I do that this cannot be done without restrictions being imposed on the individual child. But—to drop the comparison—I succeeded eventually in placing the work, in its entirety of form and content, above any details, while avoiding their violation. In this endeavour, Nietzsche's brilliant notion of 'holy sobriety', i.e. of being circumspect in one's enthusiasm, was an ever-helpful stand-by.

Let me adduce some examples to show where my problems lay. In the first place, of course, it was in those contexts where the several principal themes of a symphonic work seem to demand drastic differentiation of tempo, as for instance in Beethoven's third *Leonora* overture. In its Allegro, we find a second subject whose nobly pathetic character derives from the emotional and rhythmical sphere of the introduction, and cannot be fitted into the Allegro without a certain strain. Here, for a long time, I made a mistake that ran counter to my former weakness; sensing, quite correctly, that the fiery, energetic tempo of the first subject was the principal tempo, I tried to press the heartfelt second subject into it. Some bad performance I had heard had impressed on me its undue retardation and the obstruction this had caused in the flow of the Allegro, and trying to avoid the same mistake, I fell into the opposite one. Not until later was I able to give the melodic subject its due by a soulful delivery which yet did not noticeably abandon its *allegro* character. All the frequently encountered difficulties of this sort can be met by the above-mentioned principle of modifying the main speed impalpably and more or less gradually.

Just as the right interpretation teaches us the right tempo of a composition in which, by means of slight modifications, the musical and emotional meaning of all details can come to their full effect, so the correct tempo can help us towards the right interpretation wherever we are in doubt about the meaning of an individual phrase.

As an example of the mutual relation of tempo and interpretation, and the lessons we can draw from it, I would like to choose the first movement of Schumann's piano concerto in A minor which, often thoroughly misunderstood by its interpreters, has fallen victim to that *liberty* of speed which it is my purpose to oppose in these notes.

It is marked *allegro affettuoso*, ♩ = 84; but I call on all listeners to bear me out in my assertion that there is usually an end to the *allegro* in the fourth bar, immediately after the three fiery opening bars of the piano. Leaving the initial tempo behind, the conductor now begins the first subject at a slower speed and with a flabby, sentimentalizing expression, specially pronounced in the quavers of the second bar. This is followed by the pianist's version which is, if anything, even flabbier and weaker. And now I would ask the reader to convince himself by a glance at the score that Schumann has not provided for a change of tempo until the *forte* of the forty-second bar.

Ex. 3.

In nearly all performances, however, the *allegro* of the opening bars is not regained until this point, and then it only gives way again, after a mere six bars, to another sentimental retardation. Such an *ad libitum* approach contradicts the spirit and notation of this movement, which was furnished by Schumann with clear tempo indications, and should, moreover, be amply protected from disfigurement by its clear-cut form. This is ternary:

allegro 4/4, *andante* 6/4, *allegro* 4/4. The clarity of this form is obliterated if the lyrical variant of the main subject, which Schumann introduces in the 6/4 *andante*, is anticipated by retardation in the *allegro* of the first part, and continued in the recapitulation. Is it possible for a composer to reveal his intentions more clearly than by the three-fold notation *bewegt*, *ruhig*, *bewegt*, which, in this case, also stands for a corresponding threefoldness of emotion? This disappears entirely in the performances I am speaking of, in which the theme has freshness only in the *animato* of the *allegro*, but otherwise adheres to the emotional sphere of the *andante*.

But what if we were to follow Schumann's directions for a change? If we did, the tempo of the theme would remain exactly that of the three fiery bars of introduction; the three quavers of the second bar would be played with *élan*; and right to the entry of the soloist, a stirring, masculine character would prevail, in accordance with the direction *allegro affettuoso*. The entry of the pianist would have the same character, possibly slightly modified to comply with the calmness inherent in Schumann's direction of *espressivo*. And now, instead of the customary sentimental one, we would have an agitated rendering of this romantically dark episode:

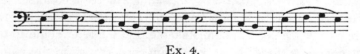

Ex. 4.

(how could a musican fail to sense its agitation?). From here on, the main speed is maintained, allowing for a slight holding back at Schumann's *un poco ritardando*, and the slight move forward at *animato*, until we reach, by way of a transitional ritardando, the *andante espressivo*, 6/4. But here the main subject undergoes a change: in pronounced contrast to its youthful, springy character in the *allegro affettuoso*, it is now calm, gentle and entranced (but here, too, the quavers should be played in time), and indulges in a tender dialogue with the clarinet, until this lyrical, *cantabile* section is suddenly ended by the return of *tempo I*, which now leads over the recapitulation into the cadenza. In this cadenza, Schumann marks the recurrence of the main subject *un poco andante*; that is, not as fast as in the *allegro affettuoso*, but not as slow as in the *andante espressivo*; his *un poco* makes sense when we look at the sixth bar whose semiquavers would lose their brilliance if we were to play them really *andante*.

Agitated passages, such as these semiquavers, often provide us with a clue to the right tempo: regard for the clear articulation of the figure-work prevents too fast a speed; their virtuoso character, on the other hand, does not allow us to take them too slowly. A tempo that is placed within such narrow limitations is easily determined, and from it, the speed of the entire phrase that contains the figuration can be readily deduced. Unless, of course, a pianist were to play the above-mentioned semiquavers as quickly as his fingers could somehow manage them, slowing down for the preceding and subsequent bars. This, too, it has been my lot to experience, and it represents the most extreme anarchy in the shaping of a tempo.

More solidly determined evidence for the choice of the right tempo than that given us by figuration is gained when we have securely grasped the speed of some specially characteristic detail of a work. Once we hold this part, we have the whole. For in almost all compositions, including those accounted less accessible, there is one passage, of a few bars perhaps, the tempo of which is quite unmistakable. Let me refer again to the F major, *forte*, bars of the Schumann concerto, as to the tempo of which there can hardly be any doubt. According to the law of continuity, this gives us the main speed of the movement which, with slight modifications, can now be applied generally, in so far as the composer has not provided for changes in speed or time-signature.

In this context, I would also like to mention a psychological phenomenon that must be familiar to every gifted re-creative musician: whenever I had been in doubt for some time about the right speed for a musical phrase or episode, it happened that I was suddenly faced with a decision coming, as it were, from a deep region of my mind; as in a moment of revelation, the right speed had dawned on me, giving me a feeling of complete certainty that took all doubt away, and remained, in most cases, with me for ever after. Characteristic of the occurrence was the suddenness of the inner dictate and the conviction of definitiveness it engendered in me. I cannot, in my own case, recall that such a perception was ever invalidated by subsequent testing; that is, by the application of the tempo thus found to the various sections of the movement.

I feel I should mention that a fantasy or rhapsody, or any piece going under whatever name, demands of us the same continuity of tempo, the same faithful regard for the intentions of the composer as a symphonically constructed movement. The fact that a piece of music may freely meander over a loosely organized design, or even appear to have an arbitrary and erratic structure, does not mean that we can give free rein to our own arbitrariness in its performance. The *Chromatic Fantasy* by Bach, however irregular, extravagant, improvisatory it may appear, has a planned design; the apparent looseness of its structure must be understood as determinate, no less than the firmly-knit fugue with which it ends, or indeed any other symphonic organism. Our rendering of a very free fantasy or rhapsody will not do justice to its improvisatory spirit until we are perfectly familiar with the piece and reproduce its meaning faithfully—we should only distort and misrepresent it if we were to superimpose our own licence on the apparent licence which the composer has seen fit to instil into it. For the *essence of all art is order*: the artistic representation of licence, and even of confusion and planless disorder, is achieved by an effort of planning, ordering creativeness, and our performance must be equally planned and ordered. In the Finale of the second act of Wagner's *Die Meistersinger*, the impression of utter pandemonium can only be achieved by careful planning on the part of a producer who has grasped the inner *law* of this dramatic scene and knows how to translate it into outward action; in this case, what is demanded by the author of the producer is the stage representation of *wild confusion*.

The fact that the freer musical forms, such as the fantasy or rhapsody, show a more frequent change of barring and tempo indications makes the law of the continuity of tempo no less binding than do the equally frequent changes in the symphonic movements of modern and contemporary composers. Continuity of flow, whether it embraces two bars or an entire movement, pertains integrally to the concept of tempo. Thus, we are nowhere given an opportunity for licence in the shaping of a tempo except at the one place where the composer himself invites us to do so: in the cadenza. Its province is a sort of musical no-man's-land, no longer subject to the laws of creativeness, yet not entirely given over to the rule of the executant. Anyhow, the author leaves us the reins here, freeing us from the obligation of the bar-line and dismissing us from service to his intentions. *Ad libitum*, he calls out to us, enjoining us to play the notes of the cadenza in our own way, like an improvisation. It is an indication of the freedom we can afford here that in the old opera until Handel it was left to the singer to compose his own cadenzas. Not so with the *recitativo*. The one in Bach's *Chromatic Fantasy*, for instance, contains, besides its cadenza-like figuration, an emotionally inspired eloquence that should oblige us to remain faithful to Bach's intentions. Then there is the recitative of the 'cellos and basses in the Finale of Beethoven's Ninth: here, the use we make of our freedom in shaping the speed must be very restricted so as not to clash with Beethoven's obvious intentions in regard to the interpretation of this passage. Provided we try to recapture the mood of the improvising composer, a *correct* performance of a piece of improvisatory tendencies, such as the bass recitative in the Ninth or the *Chromatic Fantasy*, will fully satisfy the claims of re-creative art. If, however, we were to overstress the improvisatory character by adding drastic liberties of tempo on our own part, we should have gone beyond the limits of re-creative art.

To say it once again: the concept of tempo is invalid without the correlative one of continuity. The clearest proof of this is in those very changes of tempo that are indicated by the composer. What could his *ritenuto* mean if the tempo itself were irregular? Only the fact that continuity, that is, regular flow, is an essential attribute of the concept of tempo, gives proper significance to every *ritenuto* and *accelerando, meno mosso* and *più mosso*. To be sure—'only the spirit can give life'. How little, after all, is said by these indications! No *poco ritenuto* can teach me *how* little I should retard; no *forte* how strongly, no *allegro con brio* how quickly, no *largo* how slowly I should play. These markings have only a vague, quantitative meaning which is just sufficient to point out to the interpreter the direction in which he must move to gain an understanding of the work, and save him from drastic mistakes in his performance. The indication *allegro non troppo*, for instance, will induce him to take the first subject of the first movement in Brahms' fourth symphony at a flowing but unhurried speed. The *degree* of this fluency, however, will not be clear to him until he has come to understand the character of this theme which lies between melancholy and agitation. With the right interpretation, the formerly vague and quantitative meaning of the tempo indication will gain qualitative significance—the dim light that was shed on the music by the words *allegro non troppo* brightens now to the point of a higher clarity which, in turn, will cast a new reflection on the tempo indication. Thus, it is only the right interpretation that will give us the right tempo; this latter will, conversely, make the right interpretation possible. 'One conditions the other' as Richard Wagner says. The composer, to be sure, tries his best to make us find the right tempo by his indications. But not even the apparently incontrovertible tempo indication by means of metronome-numbers can give us a reliable idea of the speed. A marking such as $\textrm{\musicalnote} = 92$ gives us a speed that may be right for the first few bars, but must needs lose its validity as soon as a change in expression demands a modification of speed. The first tempo *may* be right, as I said, but is not necessarily. For tempo is—to say it once again—essentially a qualitative concept. Strictly speaking, the right tempo can only arise from the meaning of the music; if, once in a while, we should happen to find it by the help of the metronome, this is a lucky hit.

Fortunately, the right tempo is not so rigid, in a purely quantitative sense, nor so closely wedded to interpretation, that the minutest acceleration or retardation would of necessity disfigure a musical phrase. Certainly, with a tempo that is entirely mistaken, a musical theme will wither like a plant that has not enough light or suffers under unfavourable conditions. But how—and this question sums up our difficult task—can we procure for the variegated contents of a great work the conditions of life that are appropriate for every single detail, how assemble, by means of a generally valid tempo, the frequently disparate elements of a movement to symphonic unity? We can only succeed in squaring this circle if our notion of the right tempo is of one that is elastic. And that, in fact, is the truth. If I have to conduct three performances of Bach's B minor Mass on three successive evenings, it is bound to happen that, without change in my intentions, I shall conduct the same passages at slightly varying speeds, and all three might be correct. Moreover, generally speaking, we incline in our youth to slower speeds than in old age. Which were the wrong ones? These questions can be answered once we realize that tempo is a quality which expresses itself quantitatively. By quantitative expression, I mean the degree of slowness or quickness of a tempo which, to be sure, is numerically, that is, metronomically, ascertainable; by quality, I mean the musical and emotional meaning to which the tempo corresponds. A clear interpretation of a piece, then, depends on a tempo that is determined qualitatively, but whose quantitative manifestation elastically takes account of the practical conditions of performance, while not sacrificing quality. Among these practical conditions is, for instance, the volume of sound: a larger body of strings allows a slower tempo than a smaller one; greater intensity of expression allows a breadth of speed which lesser intensity would not tolerate—and the degree of intensity may well depend on the talent, proficiency and zeal of the executant. The fact that in old age we take the same pieces faster than in our youth does not necessarily indicate a change in our conception; perhaps it only shows that mature authority succeeds in producing that same intensity of expression on which the rightness of the interpretation depends, in a more flowing tempo, where a younger man must resort to a more spacious speed.

I have stated that a tempo of given quality may express itself in slightly differing tempo-quantities. But apart from this, we must remember that there are compositions which allow for different interpretations, and that the composer himself might sometimes be ready to agree to varying conceptions of his work. This means that in all those cases where various interpretations are permissible, the variation of speed attending on them would be of the qualitative kind. Furthermore, a qualitatively unsuitable tempo, propounded with great inner conviction, may exert such persuasive force that even the composer would give it his authorization. In short: the idea of elasticity must not be excluded when we speak of the *right* tempo which corresponds to the right interpretation.

At all events, the concept of the *right tempo* stands and falls by the recognition of the principle of *apparent continuity*. If, however, neither the directions of the composer nor faithfulness to the spirit of the music can oblige us to *maintain* a tempo; if we deliberately deviate from it, obeying or disregarding the directions of the author as our fancy bids us, then anarchy will destructively descend on a domain of lofty order; and in the resulting distortion there will hardly be found a trace of the work, which was created according to a profoundly meaningful design, and should only be re-created in the same spirit.

Of rhythm

Music, the 'maiden from faraway lands' among the Muses, this non-objective, extra-mundane art, inaccessible to conceptual thinking, stands, despite its sublime singularity, in *family relationship* to other fields of art by virtue of one of its essential elements. This element is rhythm; in it, the family-ties of our art become apparent, the nearer degrees of which are evident to our sensuous perception and to our reason, while the more distant ones are suggested to us by more profound considerations.

Clearly demonstrated by rhythm is, of course, music's 'kinship of the first degree' with the dance. Musical rhythms incite and govern the rhythms of dancing; the dance derives its metrical scheme and its accents from the rhythms of music. To be sure, the total organization of music—its melodic forms, emotional content, dynamic scale, etc.—does exert an influence on the general character as well as on many diverse features of the dance; but what is decisive for the close kinship between music and dance is their unmistakable, immediate unification by a common rhythm. This union is proved immediate by the fact that its spatio-temporal manifestation is perceived jointly and simultaneously by eye and ear, and furthermore by the fact that it rests on a firm basis: the measurability of both. The dance is measurable to the extent that its movements can be exactly regulated in time, can be practised under the rule of counting and can be adapted to the metre of music. And music? Although, of its total organization, one might say with Wagner's Hans Sachs 'wie wollt' ich auch messen, was unermesslich mir schien' ('how should I measure what seemed immeasurable to me?'), yet its rhythm constitutes a measurable part of its nature which we can take hold of with certainty—in contradistinction to the intuitive manner in which we otherwise approach music's immeasurableness.

The relations between the long and short note-values of a consecutive series of notes, by which rhythm expresses itself, can be measured arithmetically. ♪. stands to ♪ in the proportion of 3 : 1, ♩.. to ♪ in the proportion of 7 : 1. ♫ ♫ ♫ is arithmetically 1½ : ½ : 1, 1 : 1 : 1, 1½ : ½ : 1. As one can see, these are uncomplicated relations between note-values which, without any effort at mathematical speculation, can be immediately perceived by anyone with a normal head for figures and sense of time. But let me add here and now the proviso that the feeling for note-values and their simple divisions is not entirely identical with the perception of these values as musico-rhythmical elements.

The meaning of rhythm—in its more restricted connotation —is expressed by short consecutive series of notes of internal unity, as for example, in the above-quoted 9/8 bar. The impression of rhythmic unity is engendered, in essence, by the accentuation of one of the notes, followed by the concomitant subordination to this note as a *thesis*[1], of some unaccented or less accented notes; the accent may, of course, as likely arise from the melodic or expressive content of the phrase as from its rhythmic sense. While it is usual for the accent to fall on a long note, leaving the short ones unstressed, it sometimes happens that interesting rhythmic formulae are created by the accentuation of a short note—the performer, therefore, has to give great attention to the question of accents and their gradation; no less important a concern is the *staccato* which, being an indispensable means for making clear the rhythmic sense of a group of notes, enables us to increase its rhythmic effect in lively manner by means of judicious gradations between sharpness and mildness. The rhythmic life of music, then, consists in the alternation of long and short, heavy and light, *tenuto* and *staccato*, and the rhythmic task of the executant lies in the appropriate gradation of these elements, and their accordance with the melodic-harmonic content of the musical phrases.

It is characteristic of the nature of rhythm that rhythmic groups such as we encounter in the metrical organization of music, may still be perceived as rhythms even when they are devoid of their melodic and harmonic components; even as mere noises, they are capable of exerting a regulating, ruling and inciting influence on the movements of dancing. Rhythms, produced on percussion instruments, accompany the dances of

---

[1] Here and below: *thesis* = strong beat, *arsis* = weak beat, in accordance with the original Greek meaning of the terms.

primitive people; even a series of noises rapped out, with strong rhythmical feeling, on a table, is apt to produce an effect that may extend into the realm of the physical. All the same, we are not dealing here with *rhythm per se*, i.e., with noises which, though they may be metrically ordered, are entirely divorced from music. Where else should this metrical order stem from, if not from a primarily musical impulse? I believe that it is a latent musical process which manifests itself in these rapped or beaten rhythms.

In the clapping of hands and stamping of feet with which keen dancers and their spectators accompany the rhythmic accents of rustic dance-music, there survives to this day something of the inner urge for giving vent to a state of musical and rhythmical excitement by way of noise-like utterances. In any case, it is clear that the lofty, non-material art of music possesses in rhythm an element whose influence extends into the realm of the physical, and which is more comprehensible, more earth-bound, more material than the other elements of music. Jazz shows this physical effect to an extreme: here, rhythm, particularly in its syncopated forms, becomes a despot under whose rule the lofty, emotional elements of music are suppressed and violated, distorted, or destroyed altogether.

There can be no doubt that the sway of rhythm over the domain of the physical springs from its affinity with the autonomous rhythmic life of our body, our heart-beat and breathing. Surely, a fiery march-rhythm or fast, exciting dance-rhythms will quicken our pulse and breathing. Does this not mean that the spiritual impact made on us by music is allied to a physical one which cannot but arise from rhythm, invigorating, as it does, the kindred rhythmic life of our body?

A somewhat more distant relationship exists between music and poetry. In the majestically flowing rhythms of the hexa-meter, in the exciting ones of dactyls and anapaests, in the inspired metres of free verse and other forms of poetry, there has manifested itself, from early epochs, a rhythmic instinct of the poet which, without doubt, is related to that of the musician.

Like the latter's, it is expressed by accentuation and by the artistically inspired alternation of long and short particles; the proportions of short and long, however, cannot be measured arithmetically in verse; they are conditioned—as are the various kinds and degrees of accentuation also—by the syllabic quantities within the words, and by the meaning and emotional content of the entire verse. If, in early medieval compositions, the accentuation and the relation of long to short in the melodic line do not conform to the laws of intra-musical rhythm, but to the verbal rhythm of the text, the reason for this must be sought in the primitiveness and narrowness of the musical idiom of that period; music was not yet what we understand by it now; its rhythmic autonomy was as yet undeveloped. It was this very development that eventually cleared the ground for our musical notation, in which the duration as well as the pitch of a note are clearly indicated; i.e., the rhythmic design is as firmly determined as the melodic-harmonic one.

In the flowing stream of that spiritual unity of melody, harmony (or polyphony) and rhythm that we call music, it is now the one, now the other element that comes to the fore. In the Adagio of Beethoven's Ninth, for instance, the lyric singing line and its noble harmonization reign supreme; by the side of these melodic-harmonic features, the relations between minims, crotchets, dotted crotchets and quavers, i.e., the mutual relations of the note-values, are scarcely felt to be a separate rhythmic process. In the Scherzo of the same work, on the other hand, we recognize that vehement rhythmic agitation is the mainspring of the movement's thematic material, development, and general form. Between these extremes lie the most variegated compounds, with one or the other element dominating; but whereas, in general, an exact, though discreet, rendering of the note-values satisfies the claims of good musical interpretation, certain pieces that are specially characterized by rhythmic vivacity, demand a corresponding regard for this quality in performance. If, then, rhythmic vivacity is an essential feature of a composition, the interpreter has to muster up energetically all his own feeling for rhythm. If he does so, it will be apparent that in a certain, not quite definable, sense, his individual rhythm will 'go beyond' the notated, measurable rhythm, thus revealing the true rhythmic sense of a group of notes which was merely adumbrated by the notation. This individual feeling for rhythm would, of course, be of no consequence if the rhythmic meaning of a musical phrase could be wholly recognized on the basis of the exact measurability of the proportions of note-values; i.e., on the basis of notation. But this is not the case—for, as suggested above, the measurability of musical rhythm, and therefore the accurateness of its notation, is only approximate. One's inborn feeling for rhythm is not concerned with numerical exactness in the relation of long to short, or short to long, as laid down by notation; it deviates from it, favouring instead an inner impulse which is compelled, instinctively, by a higher, immediate, non-arithmetical insight into the rhythmical meaning of each group of notes. It is the energy with which such spontaneous rhythms are imbued, that instils into a musical performance that spontaneity and vitality which must needs be lacking in a performance that merely aims at arithmetically measurable correctness. The latter, if held against the former, will sound quite dull. Of course, this is a question of minute differences, for the rhythm that springs immediately from our musical feeling is, as I have said, *approximately* measurable.

Divergence from arithmetical exactness occurs mainly in the case of the short notes in dotted rhythms, which an interpreter of lively rhythmic sense feels a little shorter, and therefore places a little later than prescribed by notation. Among the diverse traditions that deal with this question, I should like to mention the clear rule made by C. P. E. Bach in his *Versuch über die wahre Art, das Klavier zu spielen*[1] of shortening the short notes after a dotted note (e.g. ♪ ♪ ♪ ♪ ♩). His authority goes to prove what must seem natural to every rhythmic sense—

---

[1] *Essay on the True Art of playing Keyboard Instruments*, published in two parts, 1753 and 1762.

what good musician will not have played dotted rhythms instinctively in this manner from his youth on, glorying in such energetic execution?

It almost goes without saying that this free rendering of short notes is only feasible in a moderate tempo. At faster speeds, it would lose its meaning. But it is by no means only in the free execution of short notes in dotted rhythms that a vigorous rhythmic sense frees itself from the strict observation of notation. It will also inflect the rhythm of a waltz accompaniment by anticipating the second beat; it will augment the weight of a strong accent by a short hesitation before its entry, and so on; in short, it will defy the fetters of arithmetical correctness while making musical rhythm into a spontaneous utterance of living energy. Moreover, as mentioned above, the intuitive understanding of the time-relations between the note-values will be seasoned, by an elemental musical talent, with the two indispensable ingredients of rhythmical music-making: the accent and the *staccato*—indispensable, since without their well-graded employment, rhythm would lack its directly convincing, exciting effect.

The more sanguine a musician's temperament, the more elemental his joy in making music is, the more life-like and spontaneous will be the expression of his rhythm. For to play rhythmically means really to express one's joy in rhythm. Think of the delightful March in D major by Schubert, of the first movement of Beethoven's Seventh, of the 'March of the Janissaries' in Mozart's *Entführung aus dem Serail*, of Wagner's 'Ride of the Valkyries'—it is a sort of *joie de vivre* which expresses itself in the intuitive execution of such rhythms, and no merely intellectual grasp of arithmetical proportions obtaining in such groups of notes suffices or qualifies one for their meaningful performance. How rarely do we hear the first movement of Beethoven's Seventh performed with the rhythmical *élan* that can only arise from a spontaneous perception of ♪♫ ♪♫. One should think that the arithmetical proportion of ♪. to ♪♪ would be intelligible to anyone who 'can

count up to three'. And yet, how often does the 6/8 ♪♫
rhythm degenerate, after a little while, to 4/8 ♪.♫! A
similar painful experience is in store for the conductor in the
Scherzo of Beethoven's Ninth at the octave-skip of the strings,
which is apt to decline soon into 2/4 time. I have always made
a correct execution of the *Nibelungen* rhythm a condition of
employment with applicants for a job in an opera orchestra;
but how rarely did I find a satisfactory execution of ♪.♫ ♫♪
♪.♫! The fact is that comprehension of this dithyrambic
rhythm is only given to a dithyrambic nature; it cannot be
calculated arithmetically.

Thus we see that even the clearest possible numerical understanding of arithmetical relations between note-values is not
enough to open the door to musical rhythm; in involved cases,
it does not even guarantee a correct execution. Musical rhythm,
then, has a significance that is germane to it and qualitative,
though the lower, quantitative significance is subsumed in it.
So while an arithmetical understanding for the group ♪.♫♫
is no guarantee against its degeneration into such utterly
faulty forms as ♪.♫♫, its musically correct rendering is
readily granted to every healthy rhythmic disposition—and
that without the application of arithmetical methods. Yet the
strict measurability of note-values, though it may not suffice to
make one's performance rhythmical, remains a useful pointer in
the right direction, as well as a protection against the grosser
kinds of rhythmic mistakes. If we exclude compositions that are
mainly characterized by rhythmic vivacity, the notation of note-
values and their mutual relations is in general a reliable enough
basis for a correct rendering.

The foregoing reflections have dealt with rhythm in its
narrower sense, i.e., with the rhythmic life of music where it
determines the character of a composition. But even when it
does not predominate, rhythm is everywhere an integral part of
musical design. Every musical context has its rhythmic content,
and this brings us to the wider connotation of rhythm. Even the
quietest and most imperceptible change of note-values in the

course of a composition, even a succession of unchanging notes, as, for instance, in the chordal accompaniment of Hugo Wolf's song *Du bist Orplid, mein Land*, is a token of rhythmic life, and must be understood and designated as rhythm. Rhythm of this sort should be made distinct and comprehensible to the exact degree required by the special characteristics of a composition. To take an example, the mourning-chorus at the beginning of Gluck's *Orpheus* requires clear articulation of the even crotchets in the basses; without this the tragic character of the piece could not find expression.

A word may be said here about the influence of syncopation on the rhythmic motion of a musical passage. Its floating character counteracts any heaviness; as an *arsis*, it rebels against the tyranny of the *thesis*; by its halting gait and displaced position, and its mediation between the accents, it enriches the rhythmic life of music, which, through the more complicated forms of syncopation, may be enhanced to a state of vehement, passionate excitation.

At the beginning of this chapter, I spoke of the more distant family-ties of musical rhythm which are suggested to us on more profound consideration. I am thinking here, above all, of the cosmic rhythms, of the tides, the changes of the seasons, the motions of the planets, etc; also, of the rhythms of our bodies. Is the relation between these and the rhythms of music more than a matter of comparison? Does the rhythmic life of music reveal, perhaps, a heritage from primeval cosmic times? It is not easy for us musicians to recognize our concept of rhythm, derived, as it is, from our music, in its manifold applications to these phenomena, and to others, even more remote ones, where we find the familiar connotation of this concept transmuted almost beyond recognition. For we are well aware of the momentous significance of the fundamental distinction between the rhythms of Nature and those of Music: the rhythmic system of the body is independent of the spiritual ego; our heart-beat is involuntary and obeys natural laws; likewise, the turn of the tide and changes of season follow the laws of Nature. The musical rhythms of a composition, on the other hand, derive from the creative freedom of the composer, and undergo an inseparable union with the melodic-harmonic material to which they belong; every musical design is inherently a rhythmical one, but its rhythmic structure ensues from the free artistic imagination of man, and not from the laws of Nature which rule the rhythmic course of terrestrial and cosmic occurrences. This explains the abundance of rhythmic life in music, its attractiveness, its free alternations, untrammelled by any rules—in short, musical rhythm is an artistic concern, physical or terrestrial-cosmic rhythm a natural process.

All the same, the possibility, not to say probability, of a mutual relation must not be gainsaid. Rhythm in its widest sense is regulated temporal consecution. In this respect, there exists indeed a relationship between musical and world rhythms. Perhaps in our joy in musical rhythm, there is expressed something of the primal joy in procreation which informs the rhythmic motion of the universe.

I am well aware of the inadequacy of the foregoing considerations. The mysterious, ambiguous nature of rhythm defies verbal analysis since, as I have tried to show, rhythm is both measurable and immeasurable; a creation of artistic imagination, yet, to a limited extent, subject to mathematical laws; akin to Nature, and yet the sensitive child of the Muses. Tenuous to the point of intangibility, rhythm vibrates in music's soulful, wafted utterances, and commands as a tyrant in the wild outbreaks of its joy or sinister power; the domain of rhythm extends from the spiritual to the carnal. It is only an intuitive understanding of the extensiveness, multiformity and antithesis in the nature of rhythm that can produce that utmost vitality of performance without which the wealth and originality of a musical work cannot become living sound. The necessary basis of rhythmical music-making is the arithmetical correctness of the relations between the note-values; if they are to become an elemental rhythmic force, these relations

must be brought to life by the performer in the manner I have
indicated here.

Of clarity

My earliest musical impressions came from singing. I lis-
tened to my mother singing lieder, accompanying herself at the
piano. My father took me to summer performances of the
Kroll Opera at Berlin where I enjoyed the noble voices and
beautiful singing of Marcella Sembrich, Francisco d'Andrade
and other excellent singers in performances of operas by Mozart, Verdi and others. I used to sing to myself what I remem-
bered of impressive vocal phrases and other melodies. When I
was about fourteen, the directress and singing-teacher of the
Sternsche Konservatorium, where I was a pupil, made me
accompanist of her singing-classes; thus, I came to know the
lieder and arias in which she instructed her pupils, not only as
musical, but as technical, vocal tasks. I took part in the choir-
practices of the conservatoire, waxing enthusiastic about
choral sound; at that time, I began to frequent, as often as my
limited means permitted, the performances of the Berlin Opera.
There, in works such as *Fidelio*, and the *Magic Flute, Orpheus*
and *Der Freischütz, Rigoletto* and *Aïda*, in other operas of
various styles and in Wagner's music-dramas, I came to know
not only the vocal characters and possibilities of the human
voice, but also its dramatic potentialities. Thus, in those days,
music really meant for me the world of singing, and—perhaps
because my approach had been that of an accompanist, and I was
used, in the opera-house, to hear voices together with the
orchestra—all music appeared to my childish understanding
as a sort of melody with accompaniment. No wonder, then, that
I extended the same approach to the piano-literature with
which I occupied myself, and also to the piano-violin sonatas,
piano-trios, etc., which I played with my school-mates; in
chamber-music I made allowance, of course, for the alternation
of melody and accompaniment between the instruments. The

scores of Haydn symphonies and other classical orchestral works I approached for some time in the same naïve frame of mind.

But the fugues of the *Well-tempered Clavier* by Bach refused to respond to my notion of 'melody with accompaniment', although, to be sure, the method by which they were usually played in those days should have proved conducive to such an approach. According to this method, the fugue subject was heavily underlined, being the only important part of the composition, while the other two or three parts were dynamically completely subordinated to it, thus forming a sort of accompaniment to an ever recurring short theme. I noticed very soon that this treatment did an injustice to fugal writing, and searched for an execution in keeping with its style. As a first step, I abolished the confusing impression given by a piece in four parts that is notated on two staves, by writing it out on four staves and first playing through each part by itself, thus becoming conversant with its particular shape and realizing its relative independence; after that, I played the fugue as a whole, attempting, in doing so, to assert the meaning of each single part against the recurring fugue subject, and to adapt all parts to one another. In endeavouring to coax my fingers into a task dynamically so difficult, my sense of polyphony became gradually developed. This, again, widened and deepened my understanding of the nature of music, and gave me an altogether keener eye for the construction of music, for the relation of thematic lines to the simultaneous sounds joined to them by which they are either supported and supplemented or opposed. Soon, there dawned on me the principle of the symphonic style with its alternation of polyphony and homophony, its abundant thematic and harmonic life, its rhythmic agility, its unification of contrasting elements by a common significance, and its diversity of creative ideas out of which the entire artistic edifice grows.

As I penetrated further, the meaning of the vertical and horizontal dimensions of music became increasingly clear to me, and I felt more and more strongly the vitality and variety of the elements of a symphonic structure. In this new world, my former, naïvely unclear, notions of melody and accompaniment had gradually lost their meaning. My concept of 'accompaniment'—never understood by me in its clear verbal connotation, but rather in the confused and negative one of 'everything that is not melody'—had merged into the greater ones of polyphony and symphonic style. My concept of 'melody', however—which had originally merely comprised 'that which can be sung'—had been extended to signify a comprehensive musical line in which singable and playable elements were logically combined.

This enhanced understanding of the structure of music did not, however, have the effect of dethroning the vocal quality of my practical music-making or my instinctive attitude to music. In accordance with my native constitution and the development I have mentioned, this quality remained for me as it were the most musical manifestation of music. Thirstily, I drank in all manners and kinds of themes, in their limitless variegation: the manly, energetic ones, the passionate, agitated ones, the graceful and charming, pathetic, tender ones; yet of all themes, I was most deeply touched by those of slow movements, particularly those of Beethoven's adagios. Here, it seemed to me, the most profound secrets of music found their expression. And it was unavoidable that I should discover traces of the 'eternal feminine' in music that 'leadeth us upwards and on'[1], even far beyond the realm of slow movements—in numerous thematic configurations occurring in fast movements. In fact, every theme or motif, even the most masculine and energetic, seemed to me to show signs of its origin in the primal world of the voice; in the same way, almost all *cantabile* phrases evinced elements of vivacity and rhythmic vitality. From this instinctive insight into the hermaphroditism of musical themes which—excepting some border-line phenomena—encompasses virtually the whole thematic order, I gained for my practical music-making what

[1] The closing lines of Goethe's *Faust*, Part II.

could best be called a 'continual inclination to sing'; this, however, by no means blunted my keen sensibility for the elements of energetic masculinity found in almost all expressive contexts.

Such 'continual readiness to sing' does not merely express a certain personal leaning. That it has to be understood, in general, as an elementary gift of the re-creative musician at one with the nature of music, follows as soon as we extend the concept of 'singableness', as we may well do, to embrace the concept of the lyrical; or rather, substitute the latter concept for the former. For it would be wrong to describe as a *cantabile* theme only what we really can sing; that is, phrases that lie within the compass of the human voice. To be sure, we can also sing phrases that can hardly be called singable in any lyrical sense, such as recitatives and music of an excited, dramatic character, as for instance Telramund's outbreak of despair in the second act of *Lohengrin*, Pizarro's aria in *Fidelio*, and so on. Properly speaking, therefore, everything is singable which can and should be rendered by voice or instrument with a singing expression —*cantabile*—and this definition tallies exactly with the idea we should have of the lyrical. The domain of musical lyricism is almost boundless, and though its antecedents are no doubt vocal, this origin can scarcely be distinguished any longer in the universal significance of *cantabile*. Vast and multifarious though the realm of lyricism proper is, *cantabile* elements pass beyond it and go to inform thematic and motivic structures of an opposite character; a definitely masculine, unlyrical movement such as the first of Beethoven's Fifth, in which the second subject is the only *cantabile* excursion, must be considered an exception. The first theme of Weber's *Euryanthe* overture, on the other hand,

Ex. 5.

is an ideal example of a masculine, sharply rhythmical theme which yet contains a lyrical element of hymnic uplift. Another pertinent example is the beginning of the Rhenish symphony of Schumann:

Ex. 6.

But I am thinking, in this context, not only of such paradigms of musical hermaphroditism. Surely, we find in the general design of all symphonic movements—even in so masculine a piece as the first movement of the *Eroica*—a wealth of *cantabile* elements which must be given their due if the performance is not to wilt away in aridity. And even in passage-work, be it brilliant or dreamy as in Chopin, or elegant and gallant as in Weber's *Konzertstück*

Ex. 7.

we find a *latent* lyricism which has to be brought out in performance. Thus, we must concede to lyricism a virtual state of ubiquity in the realm of music; yet its rule is not matriarchal, for in music's husbandry the lyricism of the feminine elements is harnessed to the rhythm and dynamicism of the masculine ones, and every great musical masterpiece bears witness to the equality of those opposing forces, the interplay and discordance or concordance of which go to form the surging fullness of its content.

Among the many qualities necessary to the reproductive musician, the one we have called a 'continual readiness to sing' takes an important place—indeed the lyrical element which is well-nigh ubiquitous in the changeful design of a composition, is nurtured by this quality and would wither in its absence. But far be it from me to maintain that it is only my own approach—stemming from a youth instinct with the spirit of singing—that could lead to the sort of music-making that gives due prominence to lyricism within all expressive contexts. I can easily understand the utterly different development of a musician who has received his first impressions and stimuli from instrumental music and whose early preference was for acutely rhythmical music-making and quick, agitated compositions. For this is not a case of total opposites: my pronounced, youthful leaning towards the singable never inhibited my joy in rhythmic, energetic, or stormily agitated music; and, conversely, the existence of early preferences of an opposite character might well accord with an increasing receptiveness for the charms of lyricism. But it may have happened, during the time of my development, that my particular gifts sometimes took me in the direction of sentimentality and lack of precision in my music-making, while the opposite gifts would, at that stage of development, make for a certain dryness and harshness. But why should those two routes not meet half-way; why should their different starting-points permanently prevent mature musicians from agreeing in essentials? I am convinced that all true musicians, from whatever station they may have set out, can be of but one opinion about the intrinsic musical importance of that 'state of continual readiness to sing'.

Lyricism, notwithstanding its deep significance and vast province, represents, however, only one side of music. Music-making demands of us, beyond our readiness to sing, an abundance of talents, corresponding to the variegated and contrasting nature of music. True reproductive talent is as complex as music itself, and it is only the continual *alertness* of our entire musicality, as well as that of all our emotional and temperamental resources, that can do justice to the demands made by music on the reproductive musician.

OF CLARITY

In the first place, of course, our attention is claimed by the *principal line* which, as I have said before, continuously pursues its musico-logical course. It is here, above all, that we must show our readiness for a singing tone as well as energetic, rhythmic execution as we follow the principal line on its course through varying expressive contexts. We must be convinced that the principal line is indeed of overruling importance. For the concept of polyphony by no means includes that of the co-ordination and equality of the parts. One part may hand over to another, the principal line may lie now above, now below, now in the middle—what is essential for the interpreter's task is the fact that in most contexts there is only one principal line; to this the interpreter should give most of his attention, and to this the expression and dynamics of the other parts have to be adapted.

Does this mean, then, that despite all the arts of counterpoint and linear polyphony music is at bottom homophonic? It does indeed. Not only must the reproductive musician take this view, since clarity in execution depends on the principal line not being drowned, but always remaining audible; more than that, even the most ingenious weave of parts is intended by the composer as an organic unity—informed by a single meaning—that finds such complex expression. Musical polyphony—I crave indulgence for the paradox—is an ingenious form of homophony. That is to say, at every point of a polyphonic texture one of the parts will always be more important, to a greater or lesser degree, than the others.

This could not be otherwise, as the perceptivity of the human soul would not be equal to non-specific polyphony. It is therefore the conductor's task to provide gradations in the polyphonic texture wherever these are not indicated or effected by the instrumentation. We can test our reaction to polyphony by observing how we listen to the three simultaneous themes towards the end of the Prelude in *Die Meistersinger*: our ear is attracted chiefly by the prize-song theme in the violins and 'cellos; at the same time, we are aware of the charm of the fleet motif of the apprentices, while not taking it in quite as clearly; the mastersinger theme of the tuba and basses, too, knocks at our ear, but a little more dully still. Not even the greatest possible distinctness, the most careful dynamic balance of the three parts, will enable us to direct our attention to all three in equal measure; the prize-song theme will remain the principal line to which the others conform. I do not wish to be misconstrued as suggesting that our consciousness is strictly one-dimensional. Our receptivity is in true accord with that musical polyphony that serves a homophonic meaning. In the principal line of thinking, feeling, and perceiving taken by our spirit, other lines, engendered by simultaneous events, enter more or less powerfully; these can be interchanged with the principal line or assume its significance, but will not be exactly co-ordinated with it. This tendency towards unilinearity on the part of our perception, within its capacity for registering other, simultaneous, impressions, is demonstrated most clearly by our reactions to the complex variety of an operatic performance: at one moment, listening to the beautiful voice of a singer, we are *all ears*, hardly noticing what is happening on stage; but suddenly, a word of dramatic implications may be uttered; it takes hold of our soul, and the music that goes with it sinks to a somewhat dimmer level of our consciousness. When there is a surprising change of scene, we may at that moment become *all eyes*. In short, the principal line of our attention jumps from the singing to the scene, from the words to the action, from the domain of the ear to that of the eye; yet in our perception of the principal line, other occurrences will always play a noticeable, if less intense, role. Every sort of musical interpretation has to take account of our manner of receiving impressions by adjusting the relation between the principal line and the other parts, or whatever complex of sounds may be simultaneous with the former.

Intuitively, I had early realized the necessity for such dynamic gradations. The task was an easy one when playing the accompaniment of a song or aria, or a Chopin *Nocturne*. Here, it was really only a matter of melody and accompaniment, and everything seemed in order as long as the latter was dynamically adapted to the former, with good support in *forte*, gentle yielding in *piano*, well-adjusted *crescendi* and *decrescendi*, and carefully gradated counter-melodies and imitations. More demanding, however, were compositions of a symphonic style, such as sonatas and chamber-music works, and entirely different were works of a definitely polyphonic nature. But whether I played fugues, sonatas, or chamber-music, I always looked for the principal line, pursuing it from beginning to end and endeavouring to grade dynamically whatever went with it, and always trying to set the more important above the less important. My concern was, of course, for a higher clarity than that of sound: to wit, the clarity of musical meaning.

Nor do I know better today than to aim at, and recommend, clarity of sound by means of the gradation of simultaneous lines, according to the importance of each strand, and in nicely gauged relation to the principal line. Whether it is a case of polyphonic or homophonic style, or of an interchange between the two, such as we find in the greater part of symphonic literature—as also in piano and chamber-music, in opera and in other vocal music—the dynamic nuances and the expression of the general texture must always be adapted to the principal line and its emotional content in such a manner that the latter finds in the former the instrumental and emotional support it needs; at the same time, everything of musical importance must come to the fore without disturbing the principal line. The most intimate knowledge of a composition, and even a most heartfelt and profound performance of it, cannot have the desired effect unless we have striven for clarity by means of dynamic balance. Clarity is most decidedly one of the foremost prerequisites of musical interpretation.

The organist has at his disposal a wide array of possibilities in the differentiated use of registration and alternation of manuals. The simultaneous use of the resources of his instrument, so widely differing in volume and timbre, helps him bring clarity into the polyphonic maze of a composition, and grade the parts according to their importance.

The pianist, to be sure, only has at his disposal an instrument of uniform tone-character; and this he has to coax into differentiations of dynamics and timbre; in contrast to the organist, howeve , he has the advantage of the instrument's immediate response to touch. The fingers of a good pianist are the servants of his soul, and sensitive players have wrought miracles of dynamic differentiation in a cluster of notes. It is in this higher kind of clarity, rather than in sensual charm of tone, that the problem of pianistic touch lies; this instrument, which may at times seem so unsatisfactory, must rise in our esteem when we think of the singing *legato*, the colourfulness, and the dynamic differentiation that have been wrested by pianistic talents from the mechanism of key, hammer and string.

In the ensemble-playing of chamber-music, balance of tone is achieved thus: according as their parts are important to the whole, the single instruments will now dominate the texture, now be strongly in evidence, now be no more than audible, and now merge into the ensemble. Discussion between the players will easily lead to the desired results.

In orchestral music, however, things are very different. Here, the attainment of balance often becomes a problem, the solution of which is one of the principal tasks of the conductor. Not only does he have to bring clarity into a frequently complex texture —and that not with his own ten fingers, as the instrumentalist, but by means of the many-headed orchestral body with its instruments and groups of instruments so differentiated dynamically—he is also committed to the sound and to the sound elements which he must balance against each other, by the score of the composer. And there it may happen—and, unfortunately, often does—that the orchestration obstructs the achievement of clarity and balance. In opera and oratorio, the problem occurs in a special form: the balance between the human voice and the orchestra presents the conductor with an extremely difficult, and sometimes almost insuperable task.

For the operatic conductor, in particular, this is a *chronic* worry, which may become acute at times when he is forced to improvise a new balance for the sake of a smaller voice or an indisposed singer. On the concert platform, too, the conductor must know how to adapt orchestral dynamics to the solo instrument in a concerto, with a view to preserving the prominence of the solo violin, 'cello or piano.

I shall return to the problem of dynamic clarity in orchestral music during my discussion of conducting. Here, I wish to stress once again the great importance of clarity for every reproductive musician, and to express my conviction that clarity is the basis of musical interpretation, and must precede any attempt at emotional eloquence.

Of expression

At no time and in no place has music been merely playing with sounds. The vibrations themselves which we perceive as musical sounds are not exclusively material in nature—affective elements are active in them, lending inner meaning and coherence to the sound phenomenon: only thus can the successive and simultaneous arrangement of notes become a musical language whose eloquence speaks to the human soul. Music is not 'a sounding brass or a tinkling cymbal'[1]—the world of sound is fraught with these affective elements whose infinitely varied internal relations give spiritual significance to the successions of notes and whose tendency it is to coalesce into a special kind of affective unity: the emotional content of music. There could be no expressiveness in music if it were not inherent in the intrinsic, affective qualities of sound itself, the material of music. This elemental inclination of music towards 'feeling' explains why the musical utterances of very early epochs, long before the beginnings of our art of music, were understood as a musical language which affected the listener's emotions: in them the soul of music was latent.

[1] *I Corinthians,* XIII; set by Brahms in the last of the *Four Serious Songs.*

That musical utterances of every kind are capable of having expression, of touching the human soul, is evinced by the effect made on its listeners by non-European music, by the fact of the latter's religious use, and by reports we have of its emotional power in the communal life of distant nations. From the past, eloquent testimony has come to us as to the emotive power of Greek music, its stupendous popularity, and far-reaching influence. Plato speaks of the 'sweet and plangent harmonies which through the ear, as through a sound-trumpet, play into our souls'—where 'harmony', no doubt, stands for music in general—and mentions the effects of music, now so depressing, now so elating. Jacob Burckhardt writes of the 'heftigen und leidenschaftlichen Trauerweisen, die in Delphi auf Flöten geblasen wurden, von der Kriegsmusik, die dem Kriege, von der heiligen Musik, die dem Kultus auf Schritt und Tritt-folgte' ('violent and passionate mourning-strains that were blown by the flutes at Delphi; of the martial music, and the sacred music that closely kept pace with war and religious ceremony'), and so on.

I am mentioning these facts in order to establish the expressive power of music *per se*; that is, even of music which, like that of the Greeks, is fundamentally different from ours. Apart from the Greek scales, which we have taken over in our ecclesiastical modes, there is in our music no trace left of that powerful Greek musical art; nor is our music indebted to any non-European music, though there are occasional, external stimuli. It was through its own, inborn, impetus that our music developed from its childhood phase to its present-day position of a great power in the realm of the soul, and I am bold enough to assert that in the revelations of our music mankind has found a deeper understanding of itself, or rather, that mankind has gained through music a newer and profounder concept of the human soul. Music, in its unique, penetrating eloquence, speaks to us of depths and abysses of the human heart which none but she has been able to discover and represent. If verbal language and its development has to be considered one of the most admirable achievements of the human spirit, then we must admire, in the creation of musical language, in particular as it applies to our metrical, melodic-rhythmic-harmonic, polyphonic, symphonically conceived, subjectively intensified music, a prodigious feat of the human soul, which has learned to express itself in this music as ardently and eloquently as never before.

The increased self-knowledge and the metaphorical world-view which the genius of mankind has gained through the ascent of music to the summit of its expressive power, mark an important epoch in the essential history of man; I believe that a later age will recognize in the discovery of this *terra nova* one of the most significant events on mankind's brave march of conquest through the boundless world of spirit.

Thus the history of our music is, to a large extent, the history of expression in music. To say it again: if no affective elements were contained in sound, no expressive content could have developed in music. But it was a far way from that music whose elemental floods were propelled in a certain direction by a hidden undercurrent of spiritual origin, to music such as Wagner's Prelude to *Tristan und Isolde*. Works of this kind, though they certainly have their share of purely musical inspiration, owe their existence to a psychological need for self-expression at least as much as to the strictly musical communicativeness of their creator. From such music, there issues perceptibly and unmistakably the passionate confession of a burning heart that makes use of music as a language— here, perhaps, music may even become drowned, as it were, by expression. There exists the view—it has been taken by serious and profound musicians—that the increase of expression in music is a sign of decadence; that music had remained true to its own self only as long as it arose from purely musical inspiration, and its design and forms were determined by intra-musical considerations, while expression was not the governing power, let alone the purpose, of musical creation. From this it would follow that music had lost its purity under the increasing burden of expression, had become less and less music and more and more expression. According to this view, it was with Beethoven that this noxious transformation from a pure to an applied art, from elemental music to one in the service of expression, began.

In the first place, one might object that there has never been any expressionless music—I have pointed this out above; secondly, that the work of Bach, Handel, Haydn, Mozart, etc. offers, besides utterances of that elemental kind, music of the deepest feeling in overwhelming profusion; all their vocal music, for instance, can be considered 'pure' music, though it has been composed in every case for the sake of the expression indicated by the text, and though its inspiration has therefore been influenced, or even engendered, by expression. What does seem to begin only with Beethoven is not expression in music, but self-expression, subjectivity, self-confession. I said *'seems to begin'* advisedly, for who would assert that Mozart in the first movement of the G minor symphony or in the *adagio* transition of the G minor quintet, or Bach in the Air from the D major suite, had not spoken from their own hearts; that such music was not already the subjective, confessional manifestation of a state of soul that urged towards self-revelation? And who would consider a man of forty degenerate just because he no longer reveals the innocent purity or naïvety of a fifteen-year-old, but the maturity of soul gained by the experience of life? As the seasons of nature and the ages of man each have their particular advantages and disadvantages inherent in them, so in our music, too, the change from the stage of youth to that of maturity simply gives the impression of a development as is in accord with its character. Perhaps those periods known to man and nature as autumn and winter, fading and freezing, may be allotted to music, too. Of the music of expression, however, we can state with good reason that it represents our art's *prime of life*; the intra-musical content of the works has absorbed elements of personal and human experience; music no longer speaks of itself alone, but also of the world and mankind. As the wanderer's thoughts are gladdened and turned to home on suddenly finding traces of man in the solitude of nature—the clearing in the woods, the smoke of a chimney, the house with its garden—likewise, but more strongly and deeply, is the heart of the listener moved when he perceives in the elemental language of music the sound of the human heart which has instilled into music its own 'weal and woe'.

Emphasis on emotion in music becomes a symptom of decadence only if it is excessive, i.e. when the affective impetus has outrun musical inspiration, when the emotive significance of a piece of music outweighs its musical one. And indeed it has often happened, since the growth of music's expressive power, that composers thought they could conceal, or compensate for, the weakness of their musical endowment by the sincerity of their feelings. But whenever the invention and elaboration of a composition is not of sufficiently high musical value for it to pass muster as a piece of absolute music, whenever a work aims more at emotional than at musical effect, it belongs to the decadent class. Gustav Mahler said to me once when we were talking of the incomparably versatile creativeness of Wagner as musician, poet and dramatist: 'All being said, he remains to me most lovable as a musician'. This much is certain: whether we are dealing with Beethoven or Wagner, Mozart or Bach, Weber or Pfitzner, Mahler or Bruckner; whether it was subjective urge for confession, dramatic-poetic vision or religious fervour that inspired the musician—it is only when all inwardness has been truly transformed into music that a work of art has been born to which our love can find access. 'Transformed into music'—by this I mean that all that claimed for expression has been transferred to the lofty, artistic sphere of music, so near and dear to man. In doing this, one does not necessarily make of music's eloquence the *handmaid* of one's expressive urge—which would be equivalent to an act of *lèse-majesté*. Not at all—Schubert's music in the song *Frühlingsglaube* would touch the listener's ear and heart even without the words; it is more immediately moving than Uhland's beautiful verses if only because music altogether has a more immediate effect on the human heart. The D minor passages in the finale of *Don Giovanni* are greater than the dramatic impact of the entry of the Commendatore; and the most superb thing about the superb first act of *Die Walküre* is its musical efflorescence which is yet richer than Siegmund's and Sieglinde's overflowing bliss, for nothing can so closely entwine our soul as the blooms of music.

It is by no means my intention here to propound a sort of hierarchy in which the message of music, by virtue of its lofty origin alone, would be superior to all manifestations of beauty, profundity and wisdom of which the human spirit is capable. For I am well aware that we can find, in Goethe, Shakespeare, and Hölderlin, verses of the highest poetical beauty which, at the same time, may move and edify us after the manner of music; they might almost seem to belong to a border-district between music and poetry. Strictly speaking, verses of this sort should never be set to music since their own ethereal music can but be drowned, or disarranged by the actual music. Yet neither the near-musical effect of such rare poetic inspirations nor the especial impressiveness of artistic manifestations in any other field whatever will invalidate our assertion that music is the art in most immediate rapport with the soul. That is the secret of its incomparable influence; that is why Mozart's *Eine kleine Nachtmusik* is more enchanting to us than might be the prettiest verses capturing the romantic air of the nocturnal Salzburg scene.

To the extent to which expression has permeated music, the act of composing has increasingly become a process of transformation: emotions, poetical ideas, dramatic visions are raised up to the sphere of music, are 'transmuted into music'; thus, a work of music comes into being that is surrounded by associations from other spiritual realms; associations which, to be sure, do not diminish its unified, autonomous musicality, or intrude as foreign elements, but which enrich the work and, as it were, *humanize* it. We shall reconcile ourselves even to the illegitimate descent of so-called 'programme music' as long as the composer was musician enough to write—perhaps in spite of the programme—music that is musically inspired and cast in musically valid forms; I am thinking, in this context, of the charming second movement and the noble 'Scène aux Champs' of the *Symphonie Fantastique* by Berlioz.

I hope that it has become clear in the course of my reflections in what a comprehensive sense I am using the customarily restricted and ill-defined word 'expression'. The German *ausdrucksvoll*, like the Italian *espressivo*, connotes a lyrical quality; but the concept of expression is here extended by me to embrace everything that gives soul to music, everything that transforms the world of sound into a world of sensibility. In this comprehensive concept, there is subsumed not only lyricism, from its tenderest to its most passionate utterances, but equally the realm of the tragic, the savage, the gay, the ebullient, the grotesque, the eerie, the rousing appeal of march-music, the uplifting call of dance-music; in short, I institute here a general concept of 'expression' that comprises everything in music by which the human mind has ever been stirred, from music's beginnings to those manifestations of an unlimited, multiform, individual sensibility which the ever-intensified efforts of creative musicians have enabled music to encompass and convey.

The sublime religiousness of Bruckner's work, the romantic atmosphere of Pfitzner, and the titanic, subjective, confessional urge of Mahler's creativeness, all having contributed exciting chapters to the history of expression in music, it looks as if a certain 'de-romanticizing' of our art took place subsequently. We notice an archaistic tendency, away from emotional effusiveness, back to objectivity, to the *aural* forms of earlier music. To be sure, the historical significance of an epoch reveals itself only in retrospect, from a suitable distance in time, and it may be hazardous to interpret, from our present standpoint, the meaning of this recession after the emotional high-tide in music. Perhaps the soul of the contemporary musician has been seized by a desire for greater stillness. Perhaps our epoch is surfeited with the excitements of the wish to say 'all and every-thing'; this would give rise to an art that makes a point of sobriety. But perhaps the decrease in expressiveness is a symptom of exhaustion; perhaps, autumn is falling over the land of music; or again, this retreat from romanticism and our intentional restriction of emotionality may herald the coming of the seven lean years after the fat ones.

I do not presume to answer the Norns' question that runs 'Knowest thou what will be?'[1] But I could not forgo an opportunity of touching, however briefly, on the anxiety from which this question springs, before turning to the practical consequences which the reproductive musician must draw from a consideration of the rising curve of expressiveness in music, its calmer early days, and the incipient reversal of the last decades.

As I explained at the beginning of this chapter, music is spiritual in itself; there is, therefore, no piece of music, of any kind or from any period, for which an expressionless rendering would be appropriate. Fitted, by its nature, to be the language of the heart, music has in the course of its development eventually attained that supreme eloquence through which its messages immediately and irresistibly stir the heart of the listener. Thus, it will be seen that none but a fully emotional musical execution will do justice to the rich expressiveness of musical works. And it is equally clear that more coolness is needed in the execution of compositions of that later trend—be it called anti-romantic, formalistic, or what we will—where music has begun to rid itself of the supremacy of emotion and aspires to a new *objective* style. How warm or cool, passionate or tender, gay or sad the rendering of a piece ought to be, the quality of its expression and the degree of its intensity—the reproductive musician must deduce this directly from the composition itself. The only question is whether the complete range of emotions is at the disposal of his expressive power. We see from Wagner's essay *On Conducting*—and the memories of my own youth go to

[1] Quotation from Wagner's *Götterdämmerung*, Prelude to Act I.

72

confirm this—that the higher degrees of the expressive scale, that is, overpowering passion, ecstasy, and tragedy, rarely had a place in the interpretations of that age. In those days, the Philistine was the protagonist of the world of music, and instead of the incandescence of the emotions, which was beyond his reach, there reigned in his interpretations the tepid climate of a sluggish heart. Today, on the other hand, it is the lower degrees—calm, stillness, simplicity, ingenuousness—that seem to be missing in performances; it is as if the wish to excite the listener violently at every moment of a performance were calling into play higher degrees of the scale than is compatible with the intentions of the composer. To an ambition that aims at perpetual excitation, the stillness of those lower degrees does not exist. Whether a scale of—let us say—a hundred degrees is used only from zero to eighty or only from twenty to the top; in other words, whether it is the extremes of excitation or those of placidity that are missing in music-making, in each case the scale is too short to be fully adequate for performing, and the scope of climax-building is reduced correspondingly. I recall a performance of the C minor symphony by Brahms, in which the conductor had the first two bars of the second movement played *molto espressivo* and *mezzo forte* instead of the simple *piano* indicated by Brahms. Beginning somewhat above the middle of the expressive scale instead of in its lower regions, as no doubt intended by Brahms, this conductor not only distorted the character of the theme, but appreciably shortened the climactic range of the piece. In an age that, in contradistinction to its predecessor, inclines to excesses of expression, I am in duty bound to recommend special stillness and simplicity in the rendering of phrases thus intended by the composer. Indeed, my encouragement should be forthcoming. For in view of the struggle for maximum effect that is being waged in the concert halls of today, courage is needed to play a simply-meant phrase simply. Often, when the meaning of a phrase will in no way lend itself to exaggerations of expression or dynamics, an attempt is made to attain the desired effect by an excessive tempo. I am thinking of pieces such as the *allegro molto* finale of Mozart's *Eine kleine Nachtmusik*. How often have I witnessed the transformation of the harmless, perky jollity of the young Austrian with the flower in his buttonhole, which is summed up in this Allegro molto, into the elegant over-brilliance of a most un-Austrian and entirely flowerless *Prestissimo*!

I have discussed in the chapter on tempo how intimate is the latter's relation to expression. Here it remains for me to point out the relationship between dynamics and expression. It is usual for the more tender emotions to be expressed in *piano*: with emotional excitation, the volume increases, and it seems but natural that passion should raise its voice, and occasionally even scream. In the works of the composers who are intent on *saying everything*—from Beethoven to Strauss and Mahler—the intense pathos of emotion is usually met by an equally intense display of dynamic force. It is easy to see that the degrees of volume that correspond to the turbulent emotion of such works are altogether out of place in music of a more contained emotional cast. The dynamics of the last movement of Beethoven's string quartet in C sharp minor would be unsuitable for any *forte* passage in a string quartet of Mozart. Yet we cannot simply assume that the internal dynamicism of expression is always in direct proportion to the external volume of sound. Strength of feeling and *piano* tone are not contradictory, and solemn calm can be expressed in *forte*.

The numerous and infinitely varied types of creative genius encountered in the history of the arts seem to fall into two principal categories: the stormy, revolutionary natures, surely best exemplified by the music of Beethoven and Wagner, and the more moderate, non-revolutionary natures, as manifested in the works of masters like Bach and Mozart. I am aware that the prodigality and profusion of a work of art frequently renders doubtful its classification under the one or the other of those two styles; for, in general, living organisms refuse to be pressed into the categories which our desire for the orderly cognition of the world of phenomena tries to establish. Yet those two principal categories, despite the qualifications adduced above, and although their demarcation is not unambiguous, amount to a tolerably true representation; the significance of their fundamental opposition cannot remain hidden to the most elementary artistic sense. If I were not dealing here with music, which is in actual fact an entirely Dionysian art, I should now take recourse to the concept of Dionysian and Apollonian art in order to clarify the important stylistic distinction between the works of those two categories. For it is certain that the violent outbreaks of the style that 'has to say everything' frequently spring from the transports of impetuosity, while the works of the other class maintain *Apollonian* moderation even at climactic points. It should be evident that the difference in style between these two types of work must express itself in their respective dynamic range. The works of the first class are charged with an intrinsic emotional dynamicism which, as a rule, needs the corresponding extrinsic, that is acoustic, dynamics to make its effect. The emotional content of the 'Apollonian' works has to be expressed much less by dynamic range than by intensity and poignancy; every interpretative effort has to take account of this distinction between the two styles in regard to actual range of sound, quality of emotion, and spiritual approach. Not that these two styles have not many things in common; though the first strives for exaltation, the second for beauty, we can find beauty and moderation in Beethoven, power and exaltation in Mozart. All the same, the re-creative artist is advised to keep this difference of styles clearly before his eyes. Besides, even with Beethoven and Wagner, Mahler and Strauss, it is not always the rule that passion—as I have said above—'raises its voice': passion may whisper, mental tension may express itself in a hushed tone, discharge of tension may announce itself in powerful dynamic deployment. The words 'Für dieser Hitze heisses Verschmachten, ach, keines Schattens kühlend Umnachten' ('For this scorching fever, is there no night of cooling shade?'), in the third act of *Tristan*, have been musically expressed by Wagner with a tenseness that is well-nigh spasmodic, yet the range of moderate tone-volume is not over-stepped. On the other hand, the overwhelming *forte* of the 'Liebestod' speaks to us of liberation and redemption.

The vital diversity of musical creativeness is too extensive to be classified under a limited number of headings from which one could, in turn, derive some guiding principles for the repro-duction of each type. Not only each composer, but each single work has its particular spiritual atmosphere to which we must bring our empathy before we can do justice to it by the manner of our rendering, its gradations of intensity and the range of its emotional and dynamic scale. I stress the notion of empathy, and repeat that in central questions of expression in music the only bridge between creator and re-creator is 'from the heart to the heart'. This, surely, is the way for the executant to come to terms with his above-mentioned task of adapting the re-production of a work, in general and in particular, to its basic style. Since one can state that, generally speaking, the works in which elemental music dominates, pertain to the moderate style, and those that are governed by expression, to the Dionysian, the conclusion can be drawn that music before Beethoven demands a more moderate style of performance. But this is really no more than an approximation. As I have said, we can find in Beethoven and the composers after him works of an elemental musicality and moderate style; on the other hand, in the vocal music of the eighteenth century, and occasionally also in its instrumental music, we find excesses of expression that show how a creative genius may anticipate a later epoch.

But let us never forget that even in the most subjective 'music of expression' the personal state of mind which gave rise to it has been dissolved and transmuted into music. The re-creative artist has to approach all works, to whatever style they belong and from whatever period they come, first and foremost as a musician. If his reproduction does justice to their musical content, it will, to a large extent, have dealt adequately with the emotional content also, which, as we know, has already become music.

To a large extent—but not entirely. For the feelings, thought and mental associations that have been transmuted into music, continue to hover about this music, and *ought to do the same in its reproduction*. A performance of the third *Leonora* overture may be musically perfect, it may be intense, fiery, and powerful— but it is only when the conductor is inspired during his performance by thoughts of dark dungeons and hopelessness, of impending release and the joy of liberation, that our experience of Beethoven and his work will be complete. How could anyone hope to play *Kreisleriana* fully as Schumann intended it, if in it musical perfection and emotional intensity are not informed with that individuality of approach and mood which the interpreter can only gain from a reading of E. T. A. Hoffmann who, after all, kindled Schumann's imagination? Without the religious and spiritual elevation of the interpreter, the most musically perfect performance of Bruckner's Eighth will not come up to the composer's intentions; without a feeling for fantastic humour and solemnity, the conductor of Mahler's fourth symphony will miss a great deal.

It is different with vocal music. In Nietzsche's *The Birth of Tragedy from the Spirit of Music* we read the telling remark that music 'scatters the sparks of images'[1]; we should add that, in actual fact, music can only offer what pertains to it, has its life in it, and, as it were, seems to have been born with it; thus, what manifests itself in this 'scattering', is usually no more than an associative content latent in music. The vague relation between music and such associations is, however, consolidated to a high degree in vocal music; the expression shown by this music is interpreted by the words concurrent with it—as far as words are capable of this. To be sure, the spiritual language of music contains more expression and a different, more subjective kind of soulfulness than is offered by such words. Schubert's music to Uhland's *Frühlingsglaube*, of which I have spoken before, is filled with the emotive content of the poem, the words of which have inspired the composer to his setting. But to this Schubert's

[1] 'Die Musik streut Bilderfunken um sich'.

77

music adds its own, purely musical soulfulness and beauty; this is enhanced by the charm of Schubert's pure humanity which—like everything personal—can be expressed itself in a musical way. The rendering of a song, therefore, demands of the singer not only that he invest the vocal line with the meaning and the emotional content of the words; singer and accompanist must also, in their roles of absolute musicians, absorb the song as a piece of pure music and render it as such. For vocal music is, *pari passu*, absolute music. The more, however, music puts itself at the service of the words, becoming the mere vehicle of expressive declamation, the more decisively it divests itself of its proper power, and the more prosaic will be the effect of such vocal music. Among the most effective devices of opera is the contrast between the solely declamatory function of music in the recitativo sections—the most extreme form is the *secco* recitative, where music is just the servant of the word—and those edifices of sound in which music unfolds its full powers.

We realize that music is, in itself, spiritual. Is, therefore, unspiritual music-making ever permissible, or must not every musical utterance be accorded expressiveness? Above all, let us not underrate the importance of personality in musical execution! Its life gives life to a musical performance, its fire glows in it; surely a performance will be blunted by a dull interpreter, chilled by his coolness? Even though music, by virtue of its *inborn* warmth, may not entirely freeze to death under the breath of a frosty interpretation, there is such a thing as a virtually soulless performance, a virtually expressionless execution—as well as intentional, but misguided, 'objectivity' in interpretation—particularly with regard to compositions of earlier periods. The plain truth is that a style of objectivity, a style of interpretation that is intentionally or unintentionally soulless, or even merely impersonal, must needs do an injustice to every piece of music, for there is none that has not sprung from some elevated state of the soul. A piece like the C sharp major prelude from the first part of the *Well-tempered Clavier* by Bach expresses calm serenity in its unbroken, rolling semiquavers; the player who captures this mood will utterly charm us, while an empty, étude-like performance in the same tempo, but lacking the element of serenity, must remain ineffective.

I repeat that it is the sentiment of the interpreter alone that can decide in each case the manner and intensity of execution, that can decide whether the expression should be moderate or otherwise. One burden, above all, the re-creative artist must take upon himself: that of complete sincerity. He must not put more expression into his music-making than he feels within himself; too much 'show of emotion' is worse than too little— the latter, at worst, is a deficiency, the former a lie. It is only truthfulness that can pass 'from heart to heart'.

CHAPTER III

The Conductor

Prefatory note

I remember gratefully how as a young musician I was helped and stimulated by Richard Wagner's essay *On Conducting*. I am far from considering my deliberations as, in any sense, a continuation of, or complement to, the teachings of a creative genius. But what Wagner has handed down to us in the way of instruction is comparatively scanty; in general, advice is scarce in this wide and important field of the re-creative musician. At the same time, we must remember that in our age creative achievement in music has become of lesser, musical interpretation of greater, importance. Therefore I assume that young conductors and other readers of this may perhaps be glad to be acquainted with my professional experiences and my thoughts on conducting. Whatever the value of these insights may be, they are the result of my continuous, many-sided activity as executant, and I would rejoice in being able to give to the fruits of my life-long endeavours a profounder, supra-personal meaning and a new lease of life by putting them at the disposal of young and prospective conductors, and of all young musicians. With this practical aim in mind, I have not always been able to eschew in the subsequent chapters—as far as they deal with the special tasks or training of the conductor—an occasional didactic tone, which I have been at pains to avoid in the rest of this book. But as I felt under an obligation to make myself understood to the more inexperienced reader as well, I was compelled to address him as a person of experience. This has made necessary some digressions which the more mature among my readers are likely to find superfluous. I trust to their forbearance if, on occasion, I expatiate on matters that must for long have been self-evident to them.

An orchestral player once told Hans Richter, the great conductor of the Vienna Imperial Opera, that he had recently had his first opportunity of conducting an orchestra. 'How did it go?' asked Richter. 'Very well indeed,' replied the player; 'but you know, Herr Hofkapellmeister,' he added with some astonishment, 'this business of conducting is really quite simple!' From behind a shielding hand, Richter whispered back, 'I beg you, don't give us away!'

That conducting is not only easy, but unnecessary, was the belief of the 'orchestra without conductor' which for some time gave concerts in Russia—in Leningrad, if I am not mistaken—in which the orchestra played without the guidance of the conductor. Simultaneous entries were achieved by a gesture from one of the musicians, and ensemble-playing by thorough rehearsing and intense concentration on the part of everyone.

'Yes, but is it really of any importance who is standing up there wielding his baton?' I have, in fact, been asked. 'In the end, it is the orchestral musicians who play, give expression, and overcome the technical difficulties. Their parts, lying on their stands, tell them what to play. What more has a conductor to do than to keep them together with his movements?'

This question, as well as the naïve statement of the Viennese player and the experiment of the Russian orchestra, are based on the same assumption: that the most essential task of a conductor is beating time, and that, therefore, his is a purely mechanical function. That this in itself should be a negligible, easy, or unnecessary activity, will perhaps become doubtful to the devotees of this persuasion on attending, not the performance of some relatively simple piece, but one, let us say, of Wagner's *Götterdämmerung*, or of any symphony. But whether they believe the function of the conductor to be an easy or difficult one, an important or unimportant one, a necessary or expendable one, there remains the fundamental error of assuming that the foremost task of a conductor is to keep the players together.

This error is fostered by appearances: one sees a single person in front of all the fiddling, blowing, beating, singing musicians, and to the superficial observer, his task seems to be to bring unity and order into these masses; the eyes of all participants are directed at that one man, he raises his hand and stick and moves them, thereby keeping the many together and leading them. No wonder the 'spectator' believes such a function to be mechanical. What he does not see is the transmission of spiritual impulses from the conductor to the executants; and he does not see anything of the preceding rehearsal-work during which musical and emotional understanding has been established, either.

No one, however, who is in the least susceptible to music, will let himself be deceived by these visual impressions; his ear tells him, and his musical feeling corroborates it, that—contrary to appearances—it is in actual fact that single person who is making music, playing on the orchestra as on a living instrument, and transforming its multiformity into unity, and that he is concerned with the technical as well as the spiritual aspect of the music. The musical feeling of the listener perceives that the conductor's conception and personality sound forth from the playing of the orchestra, that his re-creative inspiration reveals, by means of the executants, the inner meaning of a work of music. The truth of this is proven by every performance under the direction of a great conductor. But even true music-lovers and connoisseurs rarely have a clear idea *how it comes about* that his personal interpretation of a composition sounds forth, perceptibly and convincingly, from a massed effort—or, in other words, what the proper sphere of the conductor's work is.

Therefore, I believe that I should try—notwithstanding the jocular injunction of the revered Hans Richter—*to give away* our professional secrets to the best of my ability. I would like to show how the general problems of musical interpretation apply in the special case of the conductor. Although my reflections are intended primarily for the young or prospective generation of conductors, they are also directed at all true music-lovers, and are meant, in particular, to satisfy those among them whose serious interest in the work of the conductor prompts them to glance into his workshop.

Peculiarities of his task

What distinguishes the activity of the conductor from that of all other musicians? That he does not play himself, but guides and influences the playing of others. It is not before he enters on the professional phase of his vocation that he can really come to know the handling of his instrument, the orchestra; practice alone will teach him to master it; only by practice can he learn.

How different it is with the instrumentalist! He has been alone with himself and his instrument during his years of study —and who would deny that one had better be alone and undisturbed when one wants to learn. He has been able to practise to his heart's content, to develop his technique, to become familiar with his instrument, to gain mastery, during years of study, of his own resources and those of his instrument.

The conductor is denied these years of quiet, preparatory exercise, in which he could become familiar with his many-sided instrument and develop his technical mastery of it. He never could, and never can, be alone with his instrument—for it consists of a great many persons—and there is no solitude among many. To him alone, of all executant musicians, is denied the inestimable advantage of being able to try out matters in the quiet of his study. Of what benefit to him are those few years of small-scale opportunities for conducting which, if all goes well, are granted to him by a friendly fate? Or even several years of wider possibilities? It is the complicated character of his instrument and indirect way in which it has to be played, and above all, the unavailability of the instrument at the time of his training, that prevent the conductor from setting out on his professional career with a degree of assurance and technical proficiency akin to that attained by other musicians.

Of correctness

Correctness is the indispensable condition and prerequisite for any musical interpretation that bears witness to the spirit and soul of a work. Exactness, cleanliness, orderliness, i.e. rightness of notes and time, clarity of sound, and compliance with dynamic and tempo indications: these are the demands of correctness, and it is only from such a basis that meaningful music-making can evolve. Even the most fiery expression cannot do justice to a passionate composition if the spirit of order is lacking in its execution, if its passages are played untidily and its rhythm inexactly. Nor can the most soulful rendering of a violin or woodwind passage make its impression unless the other instruments or instrumental groups are adapted or subordinated to it.

One may speak, by way of comparison, of the *body* and the *soul* of a musical performance, meaning by the former the actual sound that is produced by the player and makes the physical impact on the ear of the listener, by the latter the musical and emotional meaning of the performance. The saying 'Mens sana in corpore sano' can be applied figuratively to music-making: the absolute correctness of the performance stands for the healthy body from which the soul of the work, unencumbered by *physical* imperfections, can roundly and clearly sound forth.

In his elementary striving for correctness in music-making, it will become apparent to the conductor that his task is, right from the start of his career, much more involved than that of an instrumentalist. If his ear detects a wrong note he cannot, like the instrumentalist, make his own fingers put it right. Clearness in passage-work must be wrung by him from the technique of his players and not from that of his own hands. The dynamic gradation of tone, for the soloist a simple, if not always easy, task, frequently presents great difficulties to the conductor.

With the instrumentalist, the double function of execution and supervision forms an undivided and concurrent process, since in both there is at work the same ego; its powers of volition are closely geared to those of control; his own ear will teach his own hand; it will tell him instantly of mistakes in playing, and he will be in a position to correct these instantaneously, and mostly does so unconsciously. With the conductor, the striving for the same aim takes a much more complicated form—in his case, there is no organic connection between the executive and the supervisory organs: it is not with his own resources but with those of others, that he must maintain a state of bodily health in his music-making; the goal of correctness, which the soloist approaches by a direct route, must be pursued by him on circuitous paths; the homogeneity of an individual's musical powers gives place, in his case, to the endeavour to communicate with those others, the executants.

Ear and hand

It is by studying a composition, whether by way of playing it or reading it through, that the mind of the student forms an aural conception of how it should sound. Among the most important aims of studying is the gradual acquisition of a distinct, inner sound-image, or rather, sound-ideal; this will establish itself in the ear of the interpreter as a criterion that exerts a guiding and controlling influence on his practical music-making. In less independent musicians or those whose internal ear is weaker, this sound-ideal derives not from their own aural imagination, but from the impressive performances of others. Not only does the sound-ideal actively influence a performance, it has also its share in receptivity by providing a standard by which the critically listening interpreter can judge his own performance. On this dual function of the ear—namely, to give direction according to the dictates of the ideal, and to exert super-vision under its influence—depends, in actual fact, the success of every musical performance. While, with the instrumentalist, this dual function usually operates within the realm of his musical *instinct*, that is subconsciously, it must emerge into conscious-ness with the conductor: for he has to explain to his musicians in the clearest possible terms—sometimes by singing—'what is missing', i.e. in what respect his testing ear has remained unsatisfied.

The training of the ear for its two-fold task rightly belongs to one's schooling, at least as far as its first part is concerned, that is, the acquiring of vivid, inner sound-images from the study of the score. The young musician should be able, at least to a certain degree, to hear a score inwardly before setting out on his professional career. It is only afterwards, of course, that he will be able to embark on the second part of his task; of listening critically to what comes from the orchestra and of estimating in what respects this differs from his intentions.

Even when studying, the conductor must be *all ears*; in his rehearsals and performances, as I think I have now established, he must be *all ears twice over*. Technically, his achievement will depend, in corresponding degree, on his hand. Without its purposeful functioning, neither that correctness which I have called a prerequisite of spirited music-making, nor the entire gamut of lifelike tempi and expressions, the shaping of which depends on the conductor's gestures, can be attained.

Just as there is such a thing as a good piano-hand, a favourable physical disposition for violin-playing, a natural aptitude of the lips for horn-playing, there also exists a specifically manual talent for conducting, an innate skill for keeping together and guiding an orchestra by means of hand movements. The notes and indications of the score decree that the multiplicity of execu-tant musicians should become an ideal unity; the hand of the conductor makes an actual unity of them during practical music-making. His spiritual mediation, drawing inspiration from the work, is then needed to give an individual stamp to this actual, that is, sounding unity; the seal of personality must be set upon it.

The practice of every art has a basis of craftsmanship; only if he is sufficiently gifted as a craftsman and this gift has been sufficiently trained, can an artist become master of his art. If this elementary gift is lacking or has remained neglected and undeveloped, his achievement will be imperfect, even if he has considerable artistic talents. A highly talented musician without the specific gift for conducting or without technical experience, is bound to be *thrown*; the performance will come to grief, or at least not run smoothly; the orchestral players will feel insecure under his direction and will not take him seriously. The truest understanding of a work on the part of a conductor and the deepest musicality cannot make up for a lack of material correctness and technical precision in a performance—the clumsiness of the hand will prevent the work from making the right impression.

I cannot say in what specific physical trait the manual aptitude for conducting lies, any more than I can pinpoint the physical disposition for a craft such as, let us say, joinery. But if we closely watch an artisan who is specially gifted for his craft we see how naturally and purposefully, and with what sure instinct, he handles his tools. They appear to be part of his own body—his nerves do not seem to end under the skin, but seem to continue through the tool he uses, directly affecting the object on which he works. More than that, a tool is not only *innervated* but seems *inspirited* when it is employed in the service of an artistic purpose; I am thinking of the knife of a wood-carver, cutting out of the dead wood the vividly devout face and the touching posture of an apostle. The same goes for the sculptor's chisel and mallet, and similar conditions surround every tool that is wielded by the hand of a master in the service of spiritual—not necessarily artistic—purposes. But I repeat that this oneness of hand and tool, this inspiriting of the latter, can only occur in the case of an artist whom nature has granted, beside his artistic talent, that specific aptitude for craftsmanship.

THE CONDUCTOR

In the hands of the *born* conductor, the baton gradually becomes a tool of this kind. To all appearances, its function is mechanical and similar to the metronome. In reality, the beat of the metronome could never produce precise orchestral ensemble-playing just because it is purely mechanical, lacking any personal energy-impulse. The concept of musical precision has by no means only a mechanical significance; it has also a mental and qualitative significance; a beat that were nothing but mechanical could not achieve an exact ensemble, except in march-music, which, because of its regularity, is not really in need of any external direction and, besides, is held together with precision by an energy-impulse peculiar to its kind. The impulse fraught with personal energy, however, which brings to life the mechanical function of the baton and is indispensable for attaining musical precision in orchestral playing, must join hands with other mental forces before the conductor can fulfil his elementary task of achieving correctness by the wielding of his baton. For his beat is meant to achieve the musical precision of orchestral playing in the tempo conceived of as right by him, in all its ramifications as well as in *ritardando, accelerando, rubato*, etc. Such lively shaping of the tempo is among the most important requirements of musical execution; in it, the musicality of the conductor must convincingly prove itself; in the baton's function of precisely holding together the orchestra in so freely shaped a tempo, an abundance of musical and spiritual impulses must join with the mechanical gesture. This is the manner in which the tool in the conductor's hand becomes inspirited; thus it helps him in mastering his instrument—always provided that an inborn manual talent has smoothed the way towards such perfect harmony between soul and technique.

Here, some comment seems indicated on the custom of conducting without a baton, fashionable of late. Personally, I see in the renouncement of the baton the surrender of a highly developed technique of craftsmanship, which carries the seeds of decay. The baton, extending as it does the obviously restricted beat of the bare hand, and magnifying it to distantly visible proportions, provides, in view of the enhanced clarity and plausibility of its movements, a better aid to precise orchestral playing than the empty hand. Every orchestral musician will affirm that he feels much less secure under the guidance of empty hands dispensing mesmerism than under the clear beat of the baton in the conductor's right hand, which thus provides for clarity, while the left effectively looks after dynamic gradations. I regret that this technique of leading an orchestra, which has been developed to perfection, is being relinquished, and I have yet to encounter or discover conclusive arguments in favour of this. To be sure, the orchestras have got so used to stick-less hands that they are now able to follow their gestures, and I myself have heard, not without astonishment, precise performances of this sort. But I have often asked myself whether a certain crampedness and nervous restlessness frequently met with in these performances does not, at least in part, derive from the loss of that security which a baton wielded by a practised hand used to give the players. Or—to put it positively—whether it is not the *magic* of a manual direction lacking the clarifying participation of the mute tool, which produces that element of restlessness in the emotional curves of the performance? I would also like to mention that the more extended movements of the baton to left and right leave the musician in no doubt as to what beat of the bar—whether, for instance, the second or the third—is being given; this orientation, which is needed particularly in passages with frequent changes of time, can certainly not be provided with the same clearness by the empty hand as by the stick. Not to mention the directing of large forces, including orchestra and choir, as is frequent in opera: here, the more distantly posted musicians or singer will not be able to follow the movements of an empty hand with any certainty.

As to the handling of the baton, I think it is neither possible nor necessary to impart practical advice. He who has manual talent for conducting will soon wield his baton in a way that can be followed by the orchestra. It will help the beginner to watch the handling of the baton by first-rate conductors. One remark, however, I believe could be of assistance to the inexperienced: while conducting, never think of the movement of hand and baton, only of the playing of the orchestra. In the former case, one's attention would be directed at the mechanism of conducting—but this can never be an aim in itself; it is one's musical intentions rather, that should, by the skill of one's hand, be translated into movements whose mechanical meaning is wholly immersed in their musical significance as the transmitters of the impulses for expression, tempo and precision. It is to these impulses, which are in the service of one's general conception, that one's attention must be directed in conducting, even if the hand should prove clumsy and refuse to do what the head wishes. I am speaking from personal experience, for during my first years in Vienna I suffered for some time from technical shortcomings, and my mistakes only increased when I concentrated my attention upon the use of the baton. I have related in my autobiography how, in those days, every *pizzicato* chord of the strings and every freely entering upbeat of an orchestral group, was a problem to me. My difficulties became more acute the more I endeavoured to find a mechanically correct set of gestures. Experiences like these usually occur at a fairly advanced stage in the development of a young conductor, and this proved true in my case, too. For at the beginning, the technical side of conducting seems easy and unproblematic—if one has manual talent to a certain degree. I should like to put on record here that in my experience every innate talent—in music as in many other fields—usually goes through three phases of development: in the first, one can do everything; in the second, one becomes unsure of oneself, loses one's ability, searches, doubts, experiments, learns, matures; the third begins when the assurance of the first gradually returns, now enhanced and made conscious by the experience one has gained. Thus, at my début at the age of eighteen, when I conducted Lortzing's *Waffenschmied* at the Cologne opera-house, I was not aware of the slightest difficulty. I knew the score in its vocal and instrumental sections by heart, likewise the words; was thoroughly familiar with the events on stage; and had achieved, during my piano rehearsals with the singers, complete agreement on matters of music and expression. In the orchestral rehearsals and in the performances my hand took over the technical direction quite as a matter of course and I was not conscious of any difficulties; and henceforth a firm balance within the orchestra itself and between it and the stage was maintained. As far as I remember, my technical assurance in conducting lasted for some years. I was bent on gaining musical command and spiritual penetration of the works, on studying with singers and orchestra, on influencing the dramatic expression of the singers, and the stage-action; the technical function of conducting gave me no trouble since in this first phase my hand seemed to know, all by itself, what to do. My explanation of this common and deceptive phenomenon of a young conductor's unaffected assurance is that the multitude and variety of the technical problems facing the conductor, the floods of sound that inundate his ear, make such extreme demands on his powers that he cannot but be *active*: he wills, he gives, he overflows, his instinct helps, the ego operates as an undivided unity. This state of overwrought activity of course impedes the calm, critical functioning of his ear: he hears what he expects to hear, what he wants to hear—for he is entirely caught up in velleity—and it is only very gradually that his powers of judgment become equal to those of his will, that his ear learns to listen and to collate the actual sound with the standard set up by his imagination.

And thus begins—and began in my life, too—the second phase in the development of the conductor: in it the ear emancipates itself from its primitive adhesion to the complex of executive forces. This complex could only stand up against one's growing experience and self-observation, and the rising demands one makes in one's musical performances, as long as the vehemence of the active, extroverting forces was able effectively to silence one's receptivity, observation, and judgment.

It goes without saying that cruder offences against correctness or other elementary musical prerequisites have from the beginning been noticed by the conductor; these can be settled without effort by word and hand. But considerable time and ample experience are needed for his ear to develop into a superlative observer and his consciousness to shed its light on the ways of his talents and instincts. When this time arrives, he will want to account for himself, to explore the whys and wherefores of the right way. He will find himself immersed now in the unavoidable second phase of artistic development: the phase of conflict between activity and observation, when his actions have to account for themselves before the court of his self-criticism. Without such rendering of account, however, there can be no progress on the artistic, moral, or even general human plane; it is not likely that the life of any aspiring personality has ever been exempted from the crises of this period. At this time, things that have at first seemed simple often become problematic; we are no longer able to do what we used to do; our assurance dwindles, the ground wavers under our feet. This may lead to doubts in our talent threatening our vitality. The impact of this shock may differ according to the character and disposition of the person concerned; but scarcely any artist is wholly spared these growing-pains, and in some cases they may continue well into the third phase, in which conscious ability is developed. If there should be artists who have never known crises of this sort—a fact that need not be held against their talent and artistic conscience—I would have to consider their life as an exception from the law of development in three phases which, as I have said, seems to govern the growth of every talent.

This second phase, in which the hand loses its former assurance, and in which we search, err, experiment, and alternate between competence and incompetence, is essentially ruled by the tyrannical demands we make on our conducting technique in order that it may find the precision corresponding to an ever subtler shaping of the tempo. What happens is that technique is being gradually inspirited. For the freer the shaping of the tempo, the harder it is for our hand to achieve a technical precision in orchestral playing that accords with it. Sufficient natural talent provided, the spirit cannot fail to develop the technique it needs. For this is indeed essentially a spiritual task since, as I have said before, precision is only to a very limited extent of a mechanical nature—at bottom, its claims are musical, and the technique required to achieve it must, therefore, arise and evolve from spiritual-musical impulses. By concentrating on precision, one arrives at technique; but by concentrating on technique one does not arrive at precision. And as it is with precision, or rather, with that musical quality that expresses itself as precision, so it is with all musical qualities up to the subtlest and highest: if only our inner wish for them is intense enough, they will create in the course of time and experience the conducting technique that can lead the orchestra towards them. To put it more clearly: inner musical feeling is converted into technique, becomes technique. Yet this can only happen very gradually, for our intentions grow ever more refined and intricate, and our technique has to absorb refinements and intricacies in equal measure.

While, in the course of the second phase described above, the ear at last turns from a critic of technique into its helper, problems may arise from a different quarter, the like of which I myself have often found vexing and unsettling. How often I have neglected precision in my struggle for intensity of emotional expression! How often my conducting technique has failed me when I was concerned with modifications of tempo on emotional grounds to which my gestures proved unequal! Here, we are faced with an opposition that is essentially a permanent one: supreme intensity of feeling, such as is needed in music-making, will always take possession of the entire personality—thus, our emotional exaltation will diminish our attention to technical perfection, and on the other hand the striving for the latter will lessen our intensity of feeling; it is only complete mastery that is able to reconcile these opposites.

But just as, in the opera house, my advice to singers was never to force the voice for the sake of dramatic expression but rather to forgo an extreme of dramatic power for the sake of vocal technique, so I must entreat the conductor never to neglect technical perfection, even though this may lead to a compromise with expressive intensity. I am aware that this advice must sound strange coming from me; but, as I have said before, correctness is among the elementary prerequisites of music-making which must be satisfied under all conditions, for emotional effusiveness together with technical inadequacy constitutes one of the most common forms of dilettantism. My own struggle has been a long one and I speak from an experience rich in conflicts when I say to conductors: give all your soul in music-making, but never allow the transports of feeling to benumb your spirit of observation and your sense of control.

In the third phase of development, when the conductor matures towards mastery, he will be able to devote his energies entirely to the higher problems of musical interpretation, untroubled by technical difficulties. His technique, having gone during the second phase through the school of consciousness, has regained the former happy state of *unconcern*; now, however, it is on the higher level of competence. The guiding hand and the probing ear have been trained to be reliable servants of the spirit—now it is the demands of the *desiderating* ear which, having insinuated themselves, during the second phase, with growing urgency into those of the *probing* ear, govern the music-making of the conductor and his intercourse with the orchestra.

Intrinsic and extrinsic musicality

I should first make it clear that in speaking of an intrinsic and extrinsic musicality I am not referring to any clearly defined limit between intrinsicality and extrinsicality, but to the preponderance of the one or other within the totality of a musical talent. For as in music itself sensuous elements mingle with spiritual ones, so, in the exercise of music, that is, in audible music-making, intrinsic and extrinsic musicality are active in varying combinations. Musical talent has *dual citizenship*; it is domiciled in the realm of the sensuous and in the depth of the soul, and since musical talent resides in the individual, extrinsic and intrinsic musicality commingle and interact in it.

I impose no dichotomy, but merely a distinction in the interest of clarity when, in the following, I approach a definition of the facet of musical talent which I call extrinsic musicality. It is the elementary part of musical interpretation, its correctness, that largely depends on extrinsic musicality, and that to such a degree that we may state that the executant musician's profession, and above all the conductor's, is open only to talents of uncommonly strong extrinsic musicality.

Among the principal requirements of extrinsic musicality I include an excellent ear. The gift of perfect pitch is not an absolute necessity—I have known distinguished musicians who did not have it—but the perfection of so-called 'relative pitch' is. The ear must be acutely sensitive to the purity of intervals and even to the minutest uncertainty of intonation. Furthermore, the concept of aural excellence comprises utmost sensitivity for dynamic gradations and for the relations between single parts and between instruments and instrumental groups. In its wider meaning, the notion of extrinsic musicality includes facility in music-making—though intrinsic musicality has a considerable share in this: effortless music reading and playing at sight, skill in transposing; in short, the rapid comprehension of the printed page and the instantaneous translation of this impression into active music-making. A comparison between the look of an orchestral score and that of other music will readily show how much more complicated is the task of the conductor in this respect than that of other executants. Part, too, of a first-rate extrinsic musicality is the ease with which the read notes are converted into distinct inner sound images. And lastly, one of its most important features is an excellent musical memory.

Let me stress once again that facility—and that includes technical facility—is one of the principal signs of extrinsic musicality; yet the fact that musical execution comes easily to a musician, or that progress is fast during his time of training, is in itself certainly no proof of high intrinsic musicality. It is common for an excellent extrinsic musicality to master with the greatest of ease tasks which present difficulties to a higher intrinsic talent.

All practical music-making, and especially a conductor's, is, as I have mentioned, in the first place dependent on the exercise of extrinsic musicality; not even the strongest possible intrinsic musicality could bring out in a performance the essential qualities of a work unless the first-rate extrinsic musicality of the executant created the conditions for this. The popular designation for a musician who possesses all the qualities of extrinsic musicality is 'an able musician'; 'an eminent musician' is he who excels by profound intrinsic musicality. Adopting these somewhat summary popular terms, I should say that a conductor who is nothing but able can never be considered an eminent musician, but an eminent musician who is not also able can never become a conductor. But I must add, by way of reservation, that such exclusive separation is unlikely to occur frequently. With most musicians, ability and musical profundity are combined in unequal measure, and the virtues and defects of their performances depend on the preponderance of one or the other of these assets, or else on their equilibrium. *The great conductors*—and other front-rank interpreters—are those with whom ability and musical profundity are in harmonious accord; I must repeat that the most distinguished intrinsic musicality, complete with depth of emotional power, is incapable, in the absence of ability, of satisfying the requirements of a performance in accordance with the composer's intentions.

My meaning should not be misconstrued: I am not proposing to relate intrinsic and extrinsic musicality to the concepts of extrinsicality and intrinsicality in their moral connotation— I am speaking of the inner and outer domains of talent in a purely musical sense. The performance of Beethoven's *Missa Solemnis* requires a maximum of extrinsic musicality as well; Ravel's *Rapsodie Espagnole* demands the full intrinsic musicality of the interpreter for a performance in agreement with the composer's wishes. But it remains true that it is only the greatest profundity of soul and spirit that can reveal the full emotional content of Beethoven's work, whereas an excellent performance of Ravel's composition may be given by musicians in whom the spiritual is more *externalized*, provided that their general musical gifts are ample enough.

Unfortunately, I cannot follow my definition of extrinsic musicality with a complementary definition of intrinsic musicality. I have spoken before of the *outer domains* of music, and it is, strictly speaking, only these which are amenable to inspection, since some light falls on them from the world of the senses. The term 'intrinsic musicality' even indicates, perhaps, the impossibility of investigating, to however limited an extent, the dark depths of this important, if not decisive, part of musical talent. I would, however, venture to say this (though it is not a formulation, but merely a periphrasis of the truth): he to whom the realm of music is a spiritual home; he to whom, in his music-making, its language is his second—if not his native—tongue; he who understands music on hearing it like his mother-tongue: such a person has intrinsic musicality. Music makes his soul vibrate; it affects him as directly, almost, as any moving, edifying, shattering, uplifting *actual* emotional experience. What actual emotional experience is there that could touch our soul more closely than, let us say, the message of the Andante con moto in Schubert's *Unfinished Symphony*; what impress of reality could uplift it more joyfully than the Finale of his C major symphony? Music's immediate and affective impact on our soul shows how intimately related, how closely cognate are music and the soul of man. How could it be otherwise, seeing that the vast, transcendental realm of the soul harbours the springs from which music flows? The welling element of music does not only bear witness to the darkly surging recesses of the soul from which it flows; its stream also receives, and dissolves in its element, emotional impulses from the wide ambit of its fontal region. Thus there is always contained in music a latent human quality which enhances its elemental-musical impact on the plane of human experience. Schiller divined this when he said of music: 'sie weckt der dunklen Gefühle Gewalt, die im Herzen wunderbar schliefen' ('music awakens the force of dark feelings that wondrously slept in the heart').

This latent human quality in the element of music, which helps to awaken the echo of those dark feelings in the heart, must be clearly distinguished from the far less latent, sometimes even very patent, emotional and associative content whose carrier music has gradually become in the course of its history. With increasing purposefulness, the composer has filled this element, which originally was purely musical, with human experience, dramatizing it, and turning music into the proclaimer of his emotional confessions.

Surely, the practice of music must be based on intrinsic musicality since it alone finds the way to the true nature of music? In order, however, that the full strength and extent of intrinsic musicality may be actively employed and manifested in practical music-making, it must be allied to *ability*, that is, to the resources of an extrinsic musicality and highly developed technique that are in correspondence with intrinsic musicality, and together with it go to form the total talent. From this combination alone can there result a performance of musical excellence which—by virtue of the above-mentioned human elements that are suspended in the essence of pure music—will also be informed by a universal spiritual presence. And yet, to unlock all the gates of a work of music is even beyond the capacities of the master-key forged of such alloy. Ever since our art has attained to its prime of life, as I called it in the chapter on expression, i.e. since it has become an eloquent language of the soul capable of giving expression to an immeasurable wealth of feelings, capable of reflecting moods and moving our hearts—ever since then, the said combination must be supplemented by forces arising from the depth of the executant's human personality in order that not only the main-gate, but also the more recondite and internal accesses to such music may be unlocked.

The professional studies of the conductor

I shall not trouble to speak here of those studies that are part of the training of every musician, such as the theoretical subjects of harmony and counterpoint, form, composition, musical history, etc. My reflections shall deal with the special studies that are necessary for the future conductor. The first question facing us here is that of the choice of an instrument on which he could perfect himself, and which might, as his proficiency grew, offer him the most comprehensive preparation for his goal, the career of conductor.

As the real instrument of the conductor, the orchestra, will not be available to him, at best, until the latter part of his studies, and usually not until their termination—and as, in any case, he could not manage it much before—the student, in order to prepare himself for the universal tasks of conducting, must become conversant with the instrument that offers the closest possible approach of all to that universality: the pianoforte. Its range includes all audible notes; it extends from the lowest to the highest registers. Its fulness of tone provides the player with ample daily experience of dynamic nuances and contrasts; harmonic modulations and contrapuntal combinations become in practical execution—away from all theoretical studies—immediate acoustic experiences; by way of self-education and differentiation in matters of touch, the student can strive, in his own music-making, for the polyphonic clarity which he will have to achieve later with the orchestra. The relations between upper parts, basses and middle parts will impress themselves on his ear in form of actual sound, and his sense of timbre in its many shades will be fertilized and developed by his full use of the various possibilities of touch and pedalling. Furthermore, the simultaneous reading of the two staves and two clefs of piano-music is a useful introduction to score-reading; and it is only on the piano that the young musician can practise score-playing, an indispensable discipline for the prospective conductor. But above all, the literature of the piano—with its wealth of symphonic form-structures, the variety of its styles, its profusion of musical and emotional contents, its dynamic requirements—will show him the way to the future sphere of his artistic work, the province of symphonic music. There is no better preparation for the problems that await him there than that he should, with the zeal of youth, conquer as much of piano literature as he can lay hand and heart on.

Once the young musician has mastered the piano to a certain degree, it may indeed prove useful to him to acquire some proficiency on a second instrument; the best, if the most difficult, would be the violin. The care for clean intonation which demands the incessant attention of the violinist (the pianist finds intonation ready-made for him) educates and sharpens the ear; increasing familiarity with the functions of the left hand, with bowing technique, with the different tone-character of the strings, with the dynamic potentialities of the instrument— all these experiences can be of considerable advantage to the future conductor. If he can cope with it, some instruction on a wind instrument might also be profitable.

But I do not consider it an absolute 'must' to learn another instrument besides the piano. I myself have never got down to it, as my energies and time have been fully taken up by the piano and by my efforts to give myself a wider musical, as well as general, education. But I think that, with growing practical experience, I have been able to overcome the disadvantages entailed by my lack of any special knowledge of various instruments, at least to the extent of not being seriously hampered by it in my subsequent work with the orchestra.

Of the greatest importance, however, once a fair degree of proficiency has been attained in the subjects mentioned at the beginning of this chapter and in piano-playing, is the study of full scores: starting with reading exercises in the various clefs, and proceeding from the simpler to more complicated scores, the young musician should perfect himself not only in score-reading, but also in score-playing. In addition, I strongly recommend the study of Berlioz's classical treatise on orchestration. Absolutely necessary for the young prospective conductor, in my opinion, is his practical, pianistic participation in two fields: that of chamber-music and that of vocal accompaniment. Sonatas for violin or 'cello and piano, piano trios, piano quartets and quintets, are a source of most valuable experience for the growing conductor; experience, namely, in making music together. He learns to listen attentively to the other players while he himself devotes himself lovingly to the piano part. He experiences how a group of executants can become a musical unit by mutual dynamic, emotional, and general adaptation. Through his instinctive communication with the participants—now taking the initiative in the common effort, now falling in with the playing of the others, now seeking unity by means of the spoken word—the young musician gains an effective preliminary notion of the mental and spiritual task of the conductor: to make music with others, through others, and to exert his influence upon them. In striving to make his own personality felt in artistic matters, he will gradually come to know its proper strength. Besides, the wealth and distinction of chamber-music literature will, by further widening the young musician's horizon, greatly enhance and complement the above-mentioned beneficial impact of piano literature.

The understanding of the nature of stringed instruments and the refinement of his ear and sensibility that accrue to the young musician from his taking root in the noble domain of chamber music, are in need of one important supplement: if he wants to enter on his conducting career fully prepared, he must not neglect to gain thorough experience in the vocal field as well. I myself have for many years—I began as a conservatoire student—accompanied men and women singers at the piano, in songs, arias, duets and trios, and have coached them in their operatic roles; I know that my very wide experience in this field has later been of great benefit to me. It is easy to see that the acquaintance with the human voice, with singing technique and breathing, gained from such activity, is indispensable to the future conductor of opera; coaching singers in operatic roles is for him a most desirable training for his profession. But conversance with the voice and its technique, and with the blessed abundance of vocal literature, and in particular the lied, signifies far more than an important part of the operatic conductor's training: no one can—and no one ought to—perform music for whom singing is not the most musical utterance of music-making. He who cannot *sing* on the violin, the 'cello, or any other instrument, is lacking in the most important capacity of the instrumentalist. Even the pianist is not equal to his task unless he can win a *singing tone* from his, in this respect, rather recalcitrant, instrument. How then, should it not be of true advantage to every musician to imprint upon ear and soul the *cantabile* of the human voice? And again, how could he lay claim to musical culture without having approached vocal literature and the spirit of vocal music-making?

The prospective conductor who, in the interest of the universal musical education required of him, wishes to absorb the message of singing, so individual in tone and spirit, and to open his mind to the world of singing, can—to stress it once more—advance to his goal by no better route than that of assiduous music-making with singers. The knowledge of vocal literature derived from his work as accompanist or coach will not only widen his general musical education, but also show him, by numerous examples, how music is fertilized by words and their emotive content; and it will arouse and develop his dramatic instincts. No mere *studying* could replace the active, fruitful partnership of making music with singers and instrumentalists.

Moreover, it is of importance for the young musician to have practical experience of the difference between the tasks of the pianist in chamber-music playing and in song accompaniment.

To state it somewhat baldly: in chamber-music, his task is equivalent to that of the other players, in song accompaniment it is subordinate to the voice. To put it more exactly: in chamber-music, the notion of *accompaniment* has no place at all. From the concerted effort of the instruments, unity of interpretation is born; it is now this, now that player who is entrusted with the execution of the principal part, while the other players, in loyalty to the work, have to defer to him. The fact that the latter do, on occasion, become mere accompanists, does not invalidate the general principle of the equality of the instruments and their tasks in chamber-music. Conversely, even the most interesting or significant musical organization of the piano-part of a song cannot alter the fact that this part is an accompaniment, that is, subordinate to the vocal line. In other—and, for the sake of clarity, somewhat over-simplified—terms: in song, the voice is more important than the piano. This is what characterizes the pianist's task as accompanist; in this lies the peculiarity of an activity which can be of use to him with regard to his future conducting career. For the accompanist must neither approach his task as a pianist who concentrates, as in solo work, on his own playing, nor, in the spirit of chamber-music, co-ordinate his piano part with the vocal line, as in the playing of violin-piano sonatas. No, his task is to *accompany*, that is, to adapt his playing in dynamics and expression to the musical shape of the vocal line, to the meaning of the text and the composer's interpretation of it. However, accompanying by no means implies the denial of one's own personality, abject compliance, and false discretion; it demands intense empathy with the song and its singer, close identification with the whole gamut of emotions and in all dynamic nuances; for this, the wholehearted agreement of singer and accompanist is naturally required. For without that inner concord between them, no artistic achievement can result in the field of song.

The immanent law of all vocal music gives precedence to the human voice in the assembly of executants; thus the largest or-chestral forces in opera, oratorio, or sacred vocal music must be adapted, dynamically and emotionally, to the singing, just as is the piano in song-accompaniment. For the words of the text and the vocal line in which the composer has given them musical expression form the significative centre of the composition; it is, therefore, to singing, as the carrier of text and vocal line, that primacy in the performance of a vocal work is due. All the instrumental forces, complete with trumpets, kettle-drums and organ, in the Hallelujah of Handel's *Messiah*, have no other function than to enhance the splendour, the vigour, and the fire of the chorus; the apparatus is entirely in the service of the vocal purpose. Whether the work in question be Schubert's *Doppelgänger*, Brahms' *Feldeinsamkeit* or Wagner's *Götterdämmerung*, the voice takes pride of place in performance; even symphonic eloquence and polyphonic treatment of the orchestra are *in the service* of the vocal line; in a higher sense, they too become an *accompaniment* to singing; it is even true that the full, symphonic autonomy attained by the orchestra whenever the voices are silent, mostly derives its significance, and thus its law of expression, from that which had been sung and spoken; it thus remains, though intra-musically independent, in the service of the emotions, moods or actions that had been expressed vocally. Even when a solo instrument—as, for instance, the flute in the soprano aria 'Aus Liebe will mein Heiland sterben' from Bach's *St. Matthew Passion*, or the violin in the Benedictus of Beethoven's *Missa Solemnis*, or the viola in Ännchen's aria in Weber's *Der Freischütz*—rises above the ensemble to compete, as a soloist, with the human voice, the latter still holds, by word and tone, its decisively important place in the consort of executants.

Let me stress once more how important a preparation it is for the prospective conductor to play the piano in chamber-music, as a coach, and as a song-accompanist. It is song accompaniment, above all, that will provide ample practice and experience for him. In his striving for the subtlest musical 'identification' with the singer, in making lively contributions to vocal interpretation, in having regard for the singer's technical problems and his breathing, in helping him over any mistakes he might make, and again, in firmly supporting the singer by a well-held tempo and resolute rhythm and in covertly insinuating the expressive intensity of his own playing into the singer's interpretation—in all these aspects of accompanying he will find important pointers to his future tasks as a conductor.

The training of the rising musician through practical music-making is in need of an important supplement; his active endeavours must be supplemented and fertilized by training of a receptive kind: he should attend opera and concert performances and assimilate the actual sound of an orchestra. Thus, by attentive listening during performances, his silent score-reading will develop into an immediate musical experience, and his inner ear will take possession of the characteristic sound of individual instruments and of their colourful combinations. Besides, the close observation of the conductor in his work will give him many instructive hints; attendance at rehearsals, when possible, is even more illuminating—yet from the performances themselves the sensitive young musician should be able to gain —apart from important impressions of baton-technique—an intuitive understanding of the purpose of conducting and its effect on orchestra and singers.

Even a thorough and comprehensive course of studies, however, such as outlined here, combined with the greatest possible talent, cannot save the young musician from entering on the actual practice of his profession—the conducting of orchestral rehearsals and performances, dealing with the orchestra, etc. —as a *beginner*. Let him not be discouraged; we have all had to suffer these childhood complaints and growing pains; a healthy talent and unflinching will, together with patience and perseverance, always get the better of them.

The general education of the conductor

The studies of the conductor must not be restricted to music. The world of music encompasses so much of the spiritual and human—in vocal works, from the poetical and dramatic realm to that of religion; in absolute music, from the tenderest to the mightiest emotions—that the value of a conductor's artistic achievements is to a high degree dependent upon his human qualities and capacities; the seriousness of his moral convictions, the richness of his emotional life, the breadth of his mental horizon, in short, his personality, has a decisive effect on his achievements; if his personality is unable to fulfil the spiritual demands of the works he performs, his interpretations will remain unsatisfactory although their musical execution may be exemplary.

He who has not experienced the stormy sea with a feeling heart will fail to find the elemental force of expression essential for the overture of Wagner's *Flying Dutchman*, and for the landing of the ghost-ship and all the utterances of Nature in the first and third acts of the work. It is only to a romantic heart that the magic of Schumann's *Rhenish* symphony reveals itself. Beethoven's 'Scene by the Brook' will sound empty unless the conductor's own delight in a purling brook and a smiling landscape is joined to the musical soulfulness of the interpretation. None but he who is capable of dithyrambic impetus can bring to life the first movement of Beethoven's Seventh. He who is a stranger to ecstasy cannot convincingly conduct Wagner's *Tristan und Isolde*. And how shall the full stature of the Crucifixus, Sanctus, and Benedictus of Beethoven's *Missa Solemnis*, or, let us say, of the final chorus in Bach's *St. Matthew Passion*, be brought home to the listener if the conductor's heart itself be not pervaded with the lofty message of these works?

Manifold and decisive are the contributions made by the human personality of the conductor to the artistic significance of his efforts. Without the moulding of personality by the self-education of character, without the cultivation of one's general spiritual trends, without lively devotion to the interests of the mind, no course of musical studies, however zealously it may be pursued, can suffice and lead to the desired goal. To put it in a nutshell: one who is no more than a musician, is half a musician. The idea of *growing*, the striving for development, must embrace the whole inner man, and not only his musical gifts; the crown of his tree of life, his musicianship, will spread and grow in proportion as he sinks his roots firmly and broadly into the soil of universal humanity.

From two of these ramifications in particular, can strengthening sustenance reach the young musician: from Nature and Literature. What Nature may mean to the musician is avowed by the testimony and self-revelation of such works as Beethoven's *Pastoral* symphony, Haydn's *Creation* and *Seasons*, Mendelssohn's *Fingal's Cave* overture, Wagner's *Waldweben* and the introduction and many passages of *Rheingold*, Mahler's third symphony, Debussy's *La Mer*, etc. With even greater persuasion, perhaps, the profound relation of music to Nature manifests itself in such musical utterances as the moonrise at the end of the second act of *Die Meistersinger*, the Good Friday music in *Parsifal*, or the Finale of Schubert's C major symphony, this mighty symphonic piece from which, indeed, the cosmos seems to sound forth. The proximity of music and Nature is evidenced by the fact that many great musicians are intimately drawn to Nature, and that their spiritual life, and even their daily habits, are often considerably shaped by it; there can scarcely be a great musician—or a true poet—who is not charmed and shattered, inspired and uplifted by Nature, to whom her language does not speak with eloquence, and who does not feel himself her creature. This elemental allegiance of the musician cannot but exert its influence on his life as well as on his creation and re-creation: he who knows how to listen will recognize even in musical masterpieces that give no direct indication of this, the intimacy and harmoniousness of the creative musician's bond with Nature.

The mysterious relation between Nature and music reveals itself most convincingly and immediately in lieder: as, for example, in Schumann's *Mondnacht*, Schubert's *Frühlingsglaube*, Brahms' *Feldeinsamkeit*, and so on. It seems as if Nature herself were singing here, inspiring the composer, his heart at one with that of the poet, to transmute into music what flows to him from her. One can give no better advice to the young musician than that he should live with Nature: on his wanderings, he should come to know forest and meadow, hill and dale, the sunset glow and the starry night, the storm and the surging sea; he should come to feel that he is Nature's creature; he should take her spirit into his own, and enjoy a child's happiness in his attachment to her. The enrichment of his humanity that springs from these elemental experiences will, simultaneously, transform itself into musical germination.

The young musician should receive an enhancement of his entire being by familiarizing himself thoroughly with what creative spirits have thought and fancied as well as by approaching the creative spirit as it reveals itself in Nature. The great works of literature, indispensable for true culture, will open his mind to the unbounded realm of the human spirit which, as it informs all poetry, sounds forth from all music. An extensive knowledge of literature will prove fruitful in the development of the conductor's character, mind and musicality.

Whether the operatic conductor should thoroughly engross himself in dramatic literature need hardly be discussed: for the spirit of drama must permeate his musical endeavours in the interpretation of an opera. Familiarity with the works of great dramatic poets prepares the operatic conductor for the corresponding part of his task, and thus belongs to his proper province. But the absolute musician should not neglect to include the dramatic works of world-literature in his mental pabulum of occidental and oriental wisdom and poetry either; for through them he will extend his knowledge of the human heart. For the works of not only dramatic, but also absolute, music are inaccessible, in many essentials, to one who is no more than a musician; for their full understanding, they all need an amply endowed humanity as well as musical potency.

Lastly, I should like to entreat the young musician not to forget, in the course of all these endeavours, the most important thing of all: that is, to live—in the sense of having an open mind for world and man. All learning and reading would fail in its aim if it were to remain a mere accumulation of material knowledge; if it were not—like intercourse with Nature—experienced inwardly and assimilated to the ego. All the mental nourishment the conductor ingests must serve as fuel to the flame of his own spirit, as a strengthening of his independent personality. It will depend on the latter's vitality, wealth, and comprehensiveness whether his musical efforts are able to fulfil the great and numerous demands of his task.

But: 'Wer alles das merkt, weiss und kennt, wird doch immer noch nicht Meister genennt' ('Who all this has read, marked and learned hath e'en yet the name of Master not earned'). With these warning words of David in *Die Meistersinger* I would conclude my recommendations on the education of the conductor. For in one important respect, already referred to above, this path of manifold studies and endeavours is unsatisfactory, and it is necessarily so: it cannot lead the young musician to an encounter with his instrument, the orchestra, during his years of studying; it is not until his practical activity that he can come to know and learn to handle it. And in other respects, too, the scope and character of a conductor's professional tasks will cause him to feel *far from masterly* in his profession for quite some while. Moreover, his growing experience and increasing maturity will only serve to heighten his awareness of hitherto unexpected musical and personal problems in his vocation; with his achievements, the demands he makes on himself will increase. In other words, his training and education will extend over his whole life, and there will be no end to learning.

Of the practice of conducting

Let us imagine the young musician standing at last as a conductor before his orchestra, about to take his first rehearsal with musicians who are entrusted to his guidance. The step to practical conducting is made—he is beginning his career. But what he experiences now, with a fast-beating heart, is very different from the idea of an orchestral rehearsal he has dreamt about during his studies or formed from actual observation. Then, the conductor, bearing the responsibility for work and performance, had seemed to him the absolute ruler, the supreme commander of the musicians who had responded with devotion to the bidding of the practical, experienced hand of the master. But already the fast beating of his heart will not fit in with this radiant idea of kingliness: these palpitations betoken the excitement of an inexperienced person who, far removed from any dreams of sovereignty he might have cherished, and deeply troubled by his lack of routine and self-assurance, finds himself face to face with the calmness and habitual assurance of professional musicians. However thorough his general training may have been, however vivid may be his inner image of the work to be played, he is a beginner in rehearsing and conducting—above all, in rehearsing. In conducting itself, he may perhaps be helped over the first difficulties by manual skill and vigorous musicianship; the special knack of rehearsing, on the other hand, comes to the conductor only after years of professional experience. Thus the young rehearsing conductor will constantly have the sobering awareness of being a novice thrust at him. How different from what he had imagined, or experienced as a listener, does everything sound in close proximity to the orchestra—a confused and confusing jumble of sounds envelops him. What should he do or say to achieve dynamic balance and clarity? When will the right moment have come for stopping and correcting? Will he then be able to find the *mot juste*, the *right tone*, the effective approach, for gaining his musical ends with the orchestra? These and similar *acute* worries of the new conductor during his first professional contacts with the orchestra—everyone, according to his personality, will experience them in a different way—take on, after a while, a milder, *chronic* form; but they will, greatly diversified, and often assuming the proportions of serious problems, accompany the conductor over a good part of his career. For all these worries are indicative of the above-mentioned essential point of the conductor's profession, in which it differs from that of all other musicians: he has to accomplish the most personal exercise of our art, music-making, by means of exerting his influence as a man and musician on others; his task is a personal one as much as an artistic one. He who cannot deal with people or exert his influence on them, is not fully qualified for this profession.

The problem of dealing with people, as it presents itself to the conductor, can only be grasped by him if he comes to understand the profound difference of his task from that of the orchestral musicians: his is the will, theirs the obligation; and since such passive obligation, being in the nature of a depersonalization, cannot yield artistic results, it must, by means of the conductor's persuasive force upon his musicians, be transformed into willing participation.

I should advise the conductor to make himself conversant with the thought—one which should be readily intelligible to a young conductor of growing perspicacity—that every orchestral rehearsal demands of him an active effort of will-power, whereas the most he can expect of the orchestra, to start with, is a basic attitude of ready good-will and equability. To be sure, this is a relative statement, for every good orchestral musician will certainly be as keen and attentive as his task demands. This fact in itself, however, means that there will be some considerable differentiation even within the orchestra, for the soloists—the leaders of the string and wind sections, the harpist and the drummer—will be keyed up to a higher state of tension by the greater responsibility of their task than the rest of the players. The importance of the executant's task is thus a determining factor for the degree of his activity or passivity. How greatly and fundamentally therefore, must the conductor's state of mind differ from that of the orchestral musicians! Their task is, in each case, a partial one; the conductor, on the other hand, bears and feels the total responsibility for work and performance, and for the latter's spirit and details.

By reason of the high tension and activity with which this responsibility invests his whole being, the conductor will be affected in his work by the orchestra's equability—that is, its lesser degree of tension; this will be like a heavy, pressing weight, the daily shifting of which may well remind him of the lot of Sisyphus. What must come to his rescue here, is an intense empathy with the mind of the players that will teach him to put life into the orchestra, raise its tension towards his own, fire the musicians with his own fire, and kindle their activity by his.

Such empathy will help him make the orchestra into an instrument on which he can play with the freedom of a soloist. But what are the artistic means of realizing those highest orchestral achievements in which his conception, his own self, can find audible expression? I shall not trouble to try and explain the strongest and most effective means, for it is, at the same time, the most obscure: I mean by this the forcible, direct influence which the born conductor, by virtue of his inner musical intensity and the sheer power of his personality, exerts on his musicians. The forces that emanate from him create an atmosphere of spiritual communion which gives elemental spontaneity, completeness, and conclusiveness to the musical performance. Every truly sympathetic observer will have perceived in this collaboration of conductor and executants the workings of deep, instinctive forces of the soul, together with such as are elucidated by consciousness. At the very least, he will have received an intimation of an irrational element subsisting in the influence of that single one on the many.

This instinctive faculty for immediately transmitting one's own musical impulses to the orchestra is the sign of true talent for conducting. Especially in opera, where singers and chorus, too, come under its sway, it has brought about astonishing improvisatory feats of musical and dramatic expressiveness. (Opera companies in particular, incidentally, with their scheduled repeats of performances after intervals without rehearsal, have to rely on the invigorating, improvisatory flair of such conducting talents.) But our symphonic music, too, lives—as far as its life is dependent on interpretation—from the vitality of such natures. And yet, although a strong talent of this sort may be able occasionally to improvise an excellent performance without sufficient preparation, it will only in very rare, exceptional cases be in a position to dispense with thorough rehearsing. No doubt one can, from the conductor's desk, incite the participants to responsiveness, one can bring one's influence to bear on the work as a whole and in detail, one can, by the shaping of the tempo, induce the rising and falling of the emotional floods, thus reaching, moving, and shaking the souls of the listeners by way of the executants and in concord with them; yet unless the execution of details has previously been established with meticulous care, unless dynamic gradations, subtle nuances in expression, and so forth, have been thoroughly rehearsed, even the most buoyant performance will disappoint a truly musical listener. Enthusiastic scurrying over disorderly and neglected details is the hall-mark of dilettantism. If, however, a non-dilettante, but rehearsal-shy conductor makes himself guilty of this, he is behaving unscrupulously and will, in consequence, undermine the artistic morale of the executants. Loving care and impulsive intensity must be combined with unceasing industry if the demands of the work are to be satisfied in performance.

But rehearsing has a purpose yet deeper than the preparation of single performances: the gradual establishment of a musico-personal relationship between conductor and orchestra. This must sustain, supplement, and enhance the improvisatory, impelling influence of a strong conducting personality—without such increasing artistic familiarity as can only result from continuous rehearsing, the immediate influence of the conductor during performances would gradually weaken and in the end fail.

In rehearsing, then, the conductor has to give detailed expression to his musical intentions; and he must do this in a manner that will intensify the general psychological readiness of the players to fulfil these wishes.

Among the difficulties he has to overcome on his road towards this goal, one of the most serious—and it is a far more serious one than the understandable equability I have mentioned above —is the power of habit and complacency which I am constrained to call a professional disease of orchestras. How well do I remember from my first years as a conductor the frequent reply made by older musicians to my corrections: 'Well, I have always played it this way.' Whether their resistance to a change or innovation expressed itself verbally or—which was almost worse—in the passive form of standing by their convictions in hostile silence, I experienced what a great, inimical power I was challenging in my fight against habit.

There are people for whom life begins anew every morning. It is they who are ever more deeply touched by every renewed encounter with Schubert's *Unfinished*, it is they whom the perusal of a familiar Goethe poem moves with the force of a first impression; people over whom habit has no power; people who, in spite of their increasing years and experience, have remained fresh, interested, and open to life. And there are others who, when they watch a most glorious sunset or listen to the Benedictus in Beethoven's *Missa Solemnis*, feel scarcely more than 'I know this already'; and who are upset by every-thing new and unusual—in other words, people whose element is habit and comfort. It is for the former that our poets have written, our artists created, and our musicians composed; and it is for them, above all, that we perform our dramas, our operas, oratorios, and symphonies. As regards the latter, we artists must try, time and again, to burst open the elderly crust they have acquired, or with which many of them may have been born; our youthful vigour must call upon theirs or revive whatever is left of it. And in exactly this consists the task of the conductor when he deals with musicians who suffer from the said professional disease. The dull reluctance in which this disease expresses itself points to its mythical sire, Fafner, and his words: 'Ich lieg' und besitz'—lasst mich schlafen!'[1] It is exactly in his belief of possession that the error of the routinist lies. For a possession that is not being constantly striven and worked for, crumbles and melts away. There exists a habitual *espressivo* in the rendering of a musical theme as well as habitual nuances of expression in the declamation of poetry that consist in the memory of former, spontaneous interpretations and their tempo, expressive contents and fall of voice. But rendering and interpretation have gradually become stale, the live, heart-felt content has vanished, and only the manner has remained. A highly-esteemed actor once boasted to me that he was able to re-create, with the utmost success, the passionate agitation of a certain scene he had often played, without any inner participation, purely from the memory of his former performances and their points of detail, such as excessive resonance, wild gestures, sobbing, and so on. I had attended the performance which had, of course, deeply depressed me, much as I admired its virtuosity. Surely we must all realize that in artistic competence, in the mastering of the means of our art, there lurks the danger of falling into routine, and that, the more often we perform a work, the better we know it, and the more brilliant our technique has become, the more carefully we must beware of a habitual performance, and the more imperative it is for us to keep in touch with live emotion. Perhaps I may venture to instance my own life here: the more often I had to perform a work, the more care did I take to revive in myself the feeling of my first enthusiasm, and ask myself time and again whether the first spontaneity had yielded to a routined expression. There can have been scarcely a performance of *Tristan* or *Don Giovanni* or the *Eroica* in my life that was not preceded or succeeded by such self-searching—thus, the works of music ever remained for me 'glorious as on the first day'.[2] Paradoxical as it may sound, the greatness and beauty of the masterpieces

---

[1] From Wagner's *Siegfried*, Act II: 'I hold what I have—let me sleep!'
[2] 'Herrlich wie am ersten Tag': quotation from Goethe's *Faust*, Prologue in Heaven.

of all the arts is to me nothing static and definitive: they live, they *become* greater and more beautiful with every encounter, just as works of smaller stature become duller and paler. To the question whether I know Mozart's G minor symphony, I should have to answer, in all honesty: 'Today I think I know it, but tomorrow it may be new to me'; for I have often thought before that I have known it, only to find later that it was new to me.

From this ever-intensified tendency to self-examination there arose, by necessity, my resolution to carry my war against habit and indolence into the camp of my collaborators. I was hindered in this—as in every conflict of my life—by a natural tendency of mine to see how other people feel; when I put myself into the place of an *opponent*, who in this case usually waa a routined, over-worked orchestral player, it dawned on me what it must mean for him suddenly, at the bidding of a young, inexperienced conductor, to *change his ways*; that is, to play this or that in a different way from that which he had been used to and considered right. Thus, as a human being, I understood only too well what as a musician I could not tolerate, and felt, in consequence, not only artistically but also morally impeded. Besides, I realized soon enough that there was nothing in me of a Siegfried who could, sword in hand, boldly attack the dragon. I therefore essayed to find a method of rehearsing that was in accordance with my character and yet capable of over-coming the dully passive, and occasionally active, resistance of the Fafner mentality.

In this endeavour, so-called discipline could hardly be of help to me. By its application, one can suppress open opposition in the orchestra, but not silent rejection; it may uphold good manners, but cannot contribute to the artistic communication between conductor and players. Quite apart from the fact that the harsh orchestral discipline of former days has long since given place to a socially more dignified form of orderly co-operation, the concept of discipline—in its general connotation of dutiful obedience—is of a negative nature: discipline prevents disturbances. By doing this, to be sure, it creates the social basis for an artistically fruitful relation between the orchestra and its head, but the more it is stressed, the more detrimental it becomes to the spiritual rapport between them. It was really only in the most extreme cases that I made use of disciplinary measures; nearly always I succeeded in achieving order and obedience by direct, personal influence.

Here, I should like briefly to mention the traditional notion of a kind of discipline that has been found to be sufficient for regulating the relation between guidance and execution in all those cases where the higher musical or spiritual aims are not even sought after. The demands of hard-boiled mediocrity easily attain their mediocre fulfilment by means of conventional discipline.

I must, however, categorically declare myself in favour of order, in general conduct as well as in music-making itself. For the lofty intrinsic order that is an essential feature of all art and its representation, cannot be approached in an atmosphere of external disorder. An adequate degree of external discipline is as indispensable in the artistic workshop as cleanliness and orderliness are in a well-run household.

This external discipline is, however, neither able, nor supposed, to achieve more than the creation of an undisturbed atmosphere for musical work; what is needed for this work itself is the agency of an inner, higher, that is, artistic, discipline; the true supervisory power in music-making, which has scarcely more than the name in common with 'discipline'. Its province comprises attention to the directions of the composer, exactness of time and rhythm, fidelity to the laws of music in general—it is the pre-condition for the productiveness of the conductor's work with the players, and its maintenance must be his constant concern.

In order that they may be able to satisfy the practical demands of this higher, artistic discipline, conductor and orchestra are, to be sure, in need also of that special form of experience which we call routine. This last is the precious fruit from the barren field of habit: valuable, nay, necessary, since, being adjuvant to practical execution, routine renders feasible or facilitates the overcoming of such difficulties as arise in instrumental technique, sight-reading, and other tasks of the executant musician in the mastery of which experience plays a part. Routine is essential for the practical, day-to-day business of artistic institutions; but it cannot claim a higher place than that of a useful servant of musical practice—from the proper artistic sphere of music in which the spirit should reign supreme, it must most definitely be kept away.

There is no doubt that, over the years, Fafner's resistance gives less and less trouble to the conductor; it retreats before the conductor's growing experience and competence which, in turn, enhance his self-assurance; altogether, one can say that the increasing respect, sometimes mixed with fear, that the players feel for a rising personality greatly facilitates the work of the conductor with the orchestra in all its aspects. I myself, perhaps, had a particularly difficult stand with the orchestra since, as I have said, my all-too-selfless empathy in others critically reduced the assurance and energy of my self-assertion. Eventually, however, it was my very recognition of this moral impediment that showed me the way most accessible to my nature. I realized that I was certainly not cut out to be a ruler or despot, but rather to be an educator who, as we know, methodically uses his empathy with others for gaining influence over them. My task was now to enforce the powerful, nay, irresistible demands of my musical personality by means of that empathy; to uphold my own ideals uncompromisingly without violation of other people's.

In retrospect, I can state today that the artistic results of my work with singers, choirs, and orchestras in the opera-house and on the concert platform must be ascribed, if we pass over my musical and dramatic influence, to these educational endeavours. I think my musicians and singers will acknowledge that, far from being put under any pressure or compulsion, they were encouraged to obey their own inner urge in their playing and singing, and that my constant inspiriting served to stimulate them to give of their best in the common effort, and to participate in my intentions.

But far be it from me to recommend as a panacea a method that was indicated for me by my character. Every approach that enables the conductor to project himself and his musical intentions onto his collaborators has, by this very fact, proved its individual merits. Gustav Mahler, undoubtedly one of the greatest conductors of our age, effected his masterly performances by dictatorial means—unforgettable, incomparable achievements in the opera-house and on the concert-platform were wrought by his eruptive, violent personality. Strictly speaking, Mahler's results and those of kindred natures are not reached by following a method; the means employed, which are, if anything, instinctive and prompted by the moment, are revealed and justified by the loftiness of the interpretation.

But it would be a mistake to believe that I am prepared to sing the praises of despotism *per se*. For the conductor as absolute ruler is usually as much dictated as dictator; his passionate artistic intensity forces him to exert force; the demands he makes on himself are even more inexorable than those he makes on his collaborators. Besides, it is perfectly possible for this sort of artistic character to go hand in hand with goodness of heart, love of humanity, mental agility, and catholic interests, as was the case with Gustav Mahler. In its interpretative activities, such a nature is subject to an inner pressure which, in turn, compels it to seek its aims by means of subjugation.

However, it is only in extreme cases that this is a matter of apodictic contradistinction: the educator may, particularly in his younger days, develop a temperamental streak of impatience, or, when older, on occasion adopt a dictatorial attitude after mature consideration of its efficaciousness; the more violent nature, on the other hand, when dealing with very gifted or particularly obliging artists, may often be able to achieve his aims by the mildest forms of communication. Since, moreover, the methods, or 'non-methods', of influencing singers and players are not only as numerous and varied as the personalities of conductors, but also undergo development and, not infrequently, fundamental changes during a conductor's career, our sole criterion for their value will be the results they achieve: the performance. Now, it is true that I have heard excellent performances that resulted from violent methods not less often than I have encountered equally great achievements that were reached by a more educational approach. Perhaps the former were rather staggering and shattering, the latter rather uplifting and edifying; perhaps the former were mightier in their general impact, the latter richer and lovelier in details. This being so, it will depend on the specific emotional sphere of a work which conductor is more suited to it; the listener, too, will have to decide which kind of execution comes closest to his heart.

In general, however, it can be said that a violent manner of dealing with people will either be defeated by their resistance or result in their intimidation. On the other hand, the milder methods of psychological empathy, persuasion, and moral intermediation will have an encouraging and productive effect. Of course, it is more the individual effort in orchestral music-making that is favoured and promoted by these methods, whereas sharper ones often produce an amazing intensification of group-feelings, of the communal striving for achievement. The aim of the educator—in the family, in the school, and wherever human beings are entrusted to his care—is to develop the individual to his highest potentialities, to educe what is latent in him. In the music-making of an orchestra, however, is contained more than such individual efforts; apart from his individuating activity, the preponderant part of the conductor's work is in raising a community to its highest potentialities, that is, to collective efforts in which those individual elements find their organic place. Whenever, therefore, the common effort as such is to be influenced, the conductor must adapt his method to this task; his method must become as efficacious in ministering to the individual as to the collective spirit.

In these endeavours, he will experience how much easier it is to win the heart of an individual player, as for instance, the first 'cellist or the first trumpeter, than to strike enthusiasm into, shall we say, the third bassoonist or a second-fiddle player at the fifth desk. For musicians such as the latter, cited here as the representatives of the *compact majority* of the orchestra, the conductor cannot really be an educator, if education is to signify the modelling of the individual. What will be instrumental in the modelling of a group, such as is requisite here, is not any method, but rather that compelling, direct influence of the born conductor which I have instanced above as the mark of true talent for conducting; to it, the 'tutti' of the orchestra, inclusive of all second fiddlers and bassoonists, will be just as amenable as is a large meeting to the words of an eloquent leader—for strong is the binding force of group spirit, particularly under the influence of an impressive personality. Incidentally, I believe that the instinctive effect made by the conductor on the totality of musicians springs from a propensity in his nature that is, all being said, allied to that for teaching; like the conductor's educating influence on the individual, the teacher's influence is directed to the advancement of talents, and mental attitudes, and the encouragement of achievement.

A moral danger which, at the same time, is an artistic one, lies for the conductor in the power he has over others—if it is given to him, that is. It is in his interest as a human being, as well as in that of his musical achievements, to resist the temptation to misuse it. Tyranny can never bring to fruition artistic—or for that matter, human—gifts; subordination under a despot does not make for joy in one's music-making; intimidation deprives the musician of the full enjoyment of his talent and proficiency. Yet I should certainly not want to impugn the employment of earnest severity—or even the occasional borrowing of the bolt of Zeus; the latter, if the hand knows how to wield it, can in exceptional situations bring surprisingly good results. Severity is a quite legitimate, even indispensable, means of dealing with people, which the conductor cannot well forgo. But the basis of the conductor's relation to the orchestra, as of all human relationships, must be tolerant benevolence, the *bona voluntas*; combined with complete sincerity, this creates the right climate for fruitful work and will suffuse the orchestra's achievements with its warming glow.

The orchestral musician needs this warm climate for the full unfolding of his artistic abilities; under the chill of unfriendliness or mordant scorn, under the heat of impatience or anger emanating from the conductor's desk, they freeze or wither. Yet the moral force of real benevolence and sincerity is sometimes strong enough to find its way to the player's heart despite a superficially unfriendly or violent manner, whereas false friendliness or affectation, arrogance or vanity, have a vitiating, nay, destructive effect on the relation between conductor and orchestra.

If it is possible, nevertheless, for a conductor of distinguished musicianship and strong personality to achieve great, or even overwhelming results in spite of a character that predisposes him to the above-mentioned, or even worse, defects, the cause of this must be sought in a curious propensity of music: in acoustic representation, music becomes a transmitter of personality, in the sense that metal is a transmitter of heat. It transmits the ego of the performer more directly to the listener than can any other medium of direct communication from one human being to another. This explains the unequalled personal success of executant musicians of strong individuality, and their breathtaking, though transitory, impact which overwhelms the listeners and makes them oblivious of the work itself. To be sure, these enthusiasts often scarcely realize that they have succumbed not so much to the music as to the dynamism of the personality that communicated the music to them. Moreover, these mass-effects may sometimes exemplify a variation of a psychological phenomenon encountered in many other fields; namely, the urge felt by natures lacking in self-reliance to subject themselves to a strong personality. A multitude of those who are inclined to submissiveness—which may often be the cloak of worthier aspirations—respond and succumb to the tyrannical impulse to rule over the souls of others. Surely, such personal successes of certain interpreters are in no wise a yardstick of true musical culture, as a misled public opinion often believes they are. Not on successes, but on achievements, depends the standard of the public cultivation of the arts. The value of an art-offering in the opera-house or on the concert-platform can only be determined by inquiring whether this interpretation has revealed the wealth and greatness of the work and the significance of its creator. In proportion as the conductor attempts, and is capable of, satisfying this true purpose and aim of re-creation, he has proved himself the chosen apostle of creative genius and the faithful servant of his art.

At all events, personality is of decisive importance in the realm of musical interpretation, and its expansive force means more in the matter of influencing the orchestra than a spate of rational explanations. And yet, the musical achievement will be a higher one if the conductor's moral faculties allow him to be 'his brother's keeper' in relation to the orchestra, rather than its task-master. For if, to take two examples, the soli of the bass clarinet after King Marke's entrance in *Tristan*, or the themes of oboe and clarinet in the second movement of Schubert's *Unfinished* are to be instinct with the personal sentiment of these woodwind players, then the conductor must grant his players certain musical rights of their own; what is more, he must extend a helping hand to them. Wherever personal sentiment shows itself in the orchestra, it will—in careful co-ordination with the conductor's intentions—serve to enrich the performance. Conversely, if individual taste or personal, emotional participation are ruthlessly suppressed, the result will be a sort of emotional impoverishment of the performance. The conductor should strive to encourage every sign of emotional participation in the orchestra, he should explore and employ to the fullest degree the capacities of his collaborators; he should excite their interest, advance their musical talents;

in short, he should exert a beneficial influence on them. In this way, the orchestra will not be a subjugated, that is, artistically inhibited, mass of people, but a harmoniously attuned, live unity of individuals who will gladly follow the conductor's guidance; the work of art in all its facets will receive its due, and the conductor will have at his disposal an instrument from which his soul sounds forth.

The contrast between the two extremes of the re-creative character is shown by the egotistical tendency in the one case, and the selfless manner, in the other, in which the ego is affirmed. The egotist strives, consciously or instinctively, to conquer, to dominate, to triumph; that *other one*, and those *others* are for him but a means of his unlimited artistic aggrandisement, of attaining his ends with ruthless energy. Under the egotist's direction, a certain *sameness* will descend on all works; one that will detract from the wealth and variety of their creative content; but one which, at the same time, is capable of giving a strong, nay overwhelming, impression of personality. Selflessness, on the other hand, with an equal investment of personal dynamism, wishes to convince, help, advise, and teach; such an ego does not prey upon others, but seeks to give of itself to that other one, the composer, and to those others, the players, and thus to wield the influence of an educator; it means to do justice to the manifoldness of the works. The selfless ego strives to extend its power over others, the self-centred ego to incorporate others into itself. Between these two extremes in the realm of reproductive art—let us call them the conqueror and the guardian—there is, of course, every possible kind of gradation and mixture, and the resulting differentiation between the various types of musician serves to enrich our musical life. It offers to us a plenitude of works in a plenitude of different expositions, none of which is of necessity *wrong* because it differs from the others. If the talented and experienced conductor strives faithfully to explore and reveal the spirit of a work; if he, with this aim in mind, works with the orchestra in all simplicity and sincerity, the very truthfulness and seriousness of his approach will ensure that his conception shall seem no less authentic than other, different, interpretations.

I have already pointed out in a previous context that a work is capable of different interpretations and that, moreover, our own repeated performances of it need not, when allowance is made for spontaneity, entirely agree with each other. Faithfulness to the spirit knows of no rigidity—it is not faithfulness to the letter—the spirit of a work of art is flexible, *elastic*, hovering.

Once more: what matters, apart from talent, is the convictions and intentions of the conductor—his musical abilities and his character together affect the method of his practical work with the orchestra, and together they determine the artistic standard of his achievements and the strength and persuasive force of their message.

For the concert conductor

As a supplement to my foregoing reflections, there follow here —more loosely in this context—some remarks that are directed to the concert conductor in particular.

OF PRECISION. The concept of precision which, strictly speaking, belongs to the field of mechanics, has gradually made a career for itself in music, and it is the platform of the concert-hall that has become the ground of its triumphal advance. From being, quite modestly, a self-evident prerequisite of every orchestral or ensemble performance, this concept has, at least in the view of quite a few conductors, advanced to the position of a principal criterion; what is more, there is many a conductor who considers perfect precision of performance the essential part of his task. It is no wonder that in our age, dominated by technique as it is, the idea of mechanical perfection should have intruded into the realm of art, and that precision should have begun to be of overwhelming importance in the opinion of many circles. If one says of a machine that it is a precision instrument, this is praise of a factual kind; one recognizes that it fulfils one of the essential demands that can be made of a machine. But what if, on inquiring about a performance of Handel's *Messiah*, one were to be told 'It was precise'? It is possible that for the above-mentioned precisionist this would be a fully exhaustive and favourable statement about the performance; but even today, every serious and cultured musician and music-lover would conclude from the underlining of technical perfection that the performance had fallen short in essentials; that in concentrating on mechanical aspects, musical significance, religious feeling, and dramatic vitality had been forgotten or neglected; that technique had been set above spirituality, that a prerequisite had been made the ultimate end.

The fanatical precisionist quite likely will not even notice it when the mental and spiritual content of a work is being underestimated or neglected; with some justification he may even deny this to be so. For to the materialistic sense, which, like a layer of cold air, is passing from the realm of technique to our cultural zone, spirit and feeling are hardly more than illusory by-products of the material; the work is seen as a masterly musical construction, and the belief held that a performance of absolute technical precision will, by virtue of its very perfection, also contain and communicate such *nebulous elements* as spirit and feeling. Here we are faced with a fundamental error. For the bright gleam there is when a musical performance has absolute precision, is entirely of an external, not a spiritual, nature. Precision can never contain or effect spirituality; it can merely help to clear the way for spirituality to manifest itself. In all music-making, spirituality is the primary concern—that is the creed of every true musician.

Certainly, perfect precision in the playing of the orchestra and in the ensemble-work of soloists or choirs with the orchestra is an indispensable quality, and the conductor must seriously bend his energies towards attaining it; precision makes considerable and complicated demands on his technical talent, his routine, his skill and presence of mind; thus, it is in a way understandable that the numerous efforts he makes in this direction might give him a mistaken idea of the overruling significance of precision within the total of what is to be achieved. It is quite understandable, too, that the difficulties of ensemble-playing might, during his work, temporarily conceal from him the higher artistic aspects.

These difficulties result, in the main, from the manifold deviations from exact evenness in the course of a musical performance, each of which is a danger to precision; deviations such as are caused by the breathing of singers; by those—usually slight—liberties in the vocal line and in the orchestra that are conditioned by meaningful phrasing; by *rubato*; and, above all, by the agogic effects of emotional vitality, which are often considerable. Such deviations from the even flow, like exact entries—especially on upbeats—and general precision in the ensemble of large and complicated forces, should result from the conductor's educational efforts during intensive rehearsals preceding the performance; moreover, their immaculate practical execution depends on an accomplished conducting-technique.

I am not, of course, referring in the above to *deviations* prompted by licence or presumption, but to the liberties of a flexible, lively interpretation such as is congruent with true musicality and real dramatic instinct.

The fewer liberties, the easier the technical task of the conductor, but also the more inflexible and lifeless the performance. The greater the spontaneity and freedom he aspires to, the harder he makes things for himself. He may reach the point where he oversteps the limits of his technical ability and sacrifices precision to his spiritual-musical impulses; the chief loser in this is, however, not precision but the interpretation itself. For the law of precision is inexorable; it is only on the basis of an execution that is technically unobjectionable, that the spirit of a work can freely develop its full eloquence.

Therefore, a laudatory answer to the inquiry as to the performance of the *Messiah* would take, perhaps, this form: the richness, the greatness, and beauty of the music, the dramatic vitality and religious profundity of the work made their full effect; and, of course, the performance was precise, or else its musical and spiritual impact should have been impaired.

OF INSPIRITING. By inspiriting I mean the incessant impletion of music-making with expression, that is, with the vivid, ever-changing sentiment which the musical—or dramatic—consecution calls forth in the performer. Since all music originates in the soul and can never, therefore, be soulless or lacking in feeling, nothing but an unceasing inspiriting of interpretation can do justice to it. The concept 'of expression, when related to that of inspiriting, has to be taken, of course, in its widest sense; even protracted uniformity of dynamics and tempo, as for instance, in the fugato of the Finale of Beethoven's Ninth, must in no way be conceived of as being in the manner of a study, but must be inspirited by the fiery impetus of the execution. However, the injunction never to make music without inner participation, must not cause the conductor to overstate the spiritual element. Music-making requires expression, not pressure. To give more than the natural sentiment, as it is engendered by music in the interpreter, would injure the spirit of a work of art no less than to miss inner participation would. Our ideal is to let music speak for itself; we must neither distort it by a perfervid execution, nor prejudice its effectiveness by a lack of warmth. Every work of art has its proper clime; and it is in accordance with this principle that the intent, perspicacious student has to regulate the degrees of warmth or intensity in his interpretation.

I must urgently warn against perfervidness, and in general against any exaggeration of expression, which tends to rob the performance of truthfulness, turns passion into hysteria, inwardness into sentimentality, and so on. My advice is that one should rather strive for moderation and simplicity, not to say reserve.

What happened in my own case was that after my early years

of exuberance when I had the desire to 'say everything', I directed my endeavours increasingly towards moderation in the expression of emotion. This went hand in hand with a similar tendency in my personal conduct. I had, in the course of time, acquired enough insight and experience to know that every *excess* is the enemy of art, not to say a frequent sign of dilettantism; just as in daily life uncontrolled demonstrations of emotion gave me a feeling of moral discomfort. There grew up in me an ideal of *understatement* in matters artistic and mundane, which, to be sure, had to draw on a fund of sincere emotion before it could gain validity. Here, I thought, I had found that style of art and life which it was desirable to attain. The profound saying 'Art is omission' had entered into my heart, and I strove—often against my nature, which urged me to give unstintingly of all I had—to restrain myself, that is, to curb intensity of expression in music-making as far as was at all compatible with the emotional content of the music. It is a wholesome moral and artistic instinct that flinches from exaggeration in all emotional matters; I, too, was induced by it to realize my expressive intentions with the smallest possible expenditure. However, I certainly did not go so far as to suppress, continually and on principle, all show of emotion—I was only too willing to unfetter all my emotional powers when I was sure that this was the only means of fulfilling the work's requirements. Sure enough, the result of all this was an extensive emotional scale, from quiet simplicity of expression to tempests of emotionality, and I felt calm and assured in the realization that my attempts at inspiriting a work were fully sincere.

I have reported before how distressed I was, during a certain performance of Brahms' C minor symphony, by the obtrusive *espressivo* at the beginning of the second movement. This was perpetrated by a famous conductor, who apparently was so little satisfied by a simple, gentle *piano*, as is in keeping with the theme, that he preferred to substitute pathos for it. And how often I have heard the singing violin-passage in the coda of the *Lohengrin* prelude played with a similar insincere pathos, instead of p – più p – pp, *sehr feierlich* (very solemn), as noted by Wagner; how difficult it has often been for me, in my own performances, to obtain the right feeling for the solemn evanescence of this theme. The two examples cited here may stand for numerous similar cases in which routine tends to substitute a conventional, make-shift *espressivo* for the earnest sentiment that is demanded by a work.

The danger of routine, by which every reproductive musician is threatened to a greater or lesser degree according as he takes his art seriously, can be warded off more surely if one keeps in mind not only the changing course of a work's sentiments, but, above all, its general character. This gives one a sort of *basic colour* which will exert on every detail an influence that closely determines its character, i.e. is in opposition to routine. He who engrosses himself in the tragic atmosphere of Mozart's G minor symphony, and he who absorbs the fundamental mood of sunny happiness and heartfelt good spirits in Wagner's *Siegfried Idyll*, will have insured himself against an uncharacteristic clockwork *espressivo* more effectively than if, in the absence of such comprehensive ideas, he were drifting aimlessly from detail to detail. Nearly every composition gives an indication to the keen ear of the particular mental atmosphere from which it has sprung, and it is of decisive importance for the details of a re-creative achievement to recognize clearly the latter's character. I have found it useful immediately before a performance to impress upon myself again by a few characteristic words the overall atmosphere of a piece, or that of particular episodes. Such words help the conductor to regain that state of mind which should be manifested by the music.

OF CONDUCTING FROM MEMORY. There are weighty arguments in favour of conducting from memory. Every conductor fully realizes that he must know the work he performs very well indeed. He knows, or learns from experience, that he must not risk performing a work unless its musical and emotional consecution, its thematic substance, and its form and orchestration stand clearly before him; unless its totality as well as all its details 'live' within him. Such intense concentration on a work will, however, in most cases effect its spontaneous commitment to memory—I refuse to believe that one *knows a composition inside out* unless one knows it *by heart*; and it is, strictly speaking, only such thorough knowledge that qualifies and entitles one to perform a work.

From my personal experience, I should like to report that in spite of being gifted with an excellent memory, the idea of conducting without a score came to me relatively late. To be sure, during my fifty-odd years of conducting opera, I had early fallen into the habit of unwittingly conducting by heart long portions of my performances, returning to the score occasionally as the need for it arose. The frequent repetition of works in the theatrical repertoire may perhaps explain why opera conductors acquire the habit of conducting half by memory; but for me things did not change in the concert-hall for many years, although I became more and more aware of a certain distressing impediment of obscure origin. In the end, the onset of long-sightedness made me give up the score—the glasses I had to use were obscured by perspiration—and thus, a new era began in my musical life: I realized now what it had been that had so strangely impeded me in the past, and what I had shaken off by freeing myself from the sight of the music; the immediate visual contact with the musicians that was possible to me now at all times brought me hitherto unknown happiness. Nothing stood any longer between my internal image of the music and my communication with the orchestra, and I found I profoundly agreed with the remark by which Hans von Bülow, the great pioneer of our art, decisively drew the line between those conductors 'who have the score in their heads, and those who have their head in the score'.

Independence of the score seems to me of such importance for intensity and spontaneity in music-making, as also for close spiritual contact with the orchestra, that I should advise even the conductor of small retentive powers to limit himself to a few occasional glances at the music. But I must put in a warning against trying to inveigle an inadequate memory into conducting entirely from memory. A good memory is, as mentioned above, part of one's extrinsic musicality. There are distinguished, and even great, musicians with a bad memory, and mediocre ones with a quite astonishing memory. Therefore, I should advise anyone who cannot trust his memory with absolute certainty, to have no qualms about putting the score on his desk while, however, not making more use of it than is absolutely necessary. In rehearsals, to be sure, the score is indispensable, if only because it has to be consulted when an orchestral part gives room for doubt, and for the benefit of the figures and letters which enable conductor and players to resume their work after interruptions without delay.

There are conductors whose memory retains even these figures and letters. Here, however, it is not musical, but visual, memory that is at work. It is the appearance of the score's pages, together with these symbols, that has impressed itself upon the visual sense, but this feat of memory, however astonishing it may be, has no musical significance at all. It is exclusively the memory of the aural sense which is apt to have such beneficial effects on the conductor's artistic achievement; he conducts, while his inner ear now expects the entry of the bassoon on the third crotchet, now anticipates the bass-note of the harp on the first crotchet, now envisages the imminent upbeat in the violas, and so on. All this lives in his musical memory and emerges from it at the right moment, perhaps accompanied by a visual image of the score, but called forth by the living, inner aural image of the work and its progress during performance. It is this reliable musical memory that, by intensive study, makes itself master of the work, and henceforth allows the conductor to be in uninterrupted spiritual contact with the executants—players, soloists, choirs. The above-mentioned irrational element that has its part in the conductor's influence on these, depends on his seeing *eye to eye* with them, and I take leave to doubt whether a conductor who has his head in the score, will be able to instil his impulses into all the spiritual forces surrounding him.

OF DYNAMICS. Among the foremost tasks of the conductor is the care for clarity of each orchestral part and dynamic balance within the ensemble of the orchestra. All that is significant, beautiful, and moving in the message of music can only become comprehensive and impressive if it is pronounced with clarity. Whether the task of attaining this clarity is an easy or difficult one for the conductor depends, apart from his talent and competence, on the instrumentation. There exist scores, simple as well as complex ones, where a thorough knowledge of the orchestra has provided so wisely for clarity and dynamic balance that this aspect of the conductor's task—to discount the others for the moment—offers no problems. Yet he often has to deal with other works—even some of high distinction—whose instrumentation can be translated into distinct sound only with great difficulty, either because the composer did not know the orchestra well enough or because he did not concentrate his efforts on such clarity of sound.

Dynamic problems frequently arise, of course, from the difference in volume between the instruments or groups of the orchestra; strings and woodwind are hopelessly inferior in strength to brass and percussion; within the brass-group, again, trumpets and trombones have a much bigger tone than the horns, and the massed strings are apt to drown the woodwind. In calm and *piano* passages, dynamic balance can usually be achieved without difficulty. In excited passages and in *forte*, however, the contest of voices in the orchestral family will become a babel of confusion; the right of the stronger will rudely prevail unless a musically meaningful compromise between the contesting sonorities is brought about by planned care in orchestration and dynamic markings, or by the ordering authority of the conductor.

Nor will his most eager and expert attention during rehearsals be at all sufficient for securing dynamic balance in the playing of the orchestra. During the performance itself the conductor will still have to exert himself to ensure the supremacy of main parts and the subordination or adaptation of others. The countless sound-combinations of the orchestra require, as well as thorough preparatory work, the subtlest supervision and actual control in performance if the clear continuity of the melos is to be attained. The dynamic directions of the conductor during rehearsals will have to be supplemented by the underlining or effacing gestures of his hand during the performance. Within these diverse and manifold cares of the conductor for the clear continuity of the melos on all dynamic levels, there is one chief problem that occupies the conductor in all contexts: the treatment of brass and percussion and, in particular, of natural instruments and kettle-drums in the *forte* passages of classical music. According to the intentions of classical composers, the *forte* of natural horns and trumpets is meant to give vigour and brilliance to that of the whole orchestra, and it is the task of the conductor to fulfil this demand without disturbing or encumbering the main melodic lines of strings or woodwind by the volume of those non-melodic notes. The composers have made this difficult for us, and even Mozart, that profound connoisseur of the orchestra and master of orchestration, has, by his summary *forte* directions for trumpets, horns, and kettledrums in energetic passages, posed a difficult task to the aural sense of the conductor and his endeavours for clarity; examples of this are the first and last movement of the *Jupiter* symphony, the overtures of *Don Giovanni* and *Figaro*; there are many others.

My first encounter with this problem dates from my early youth and has been of lasting influence on my entire career: as a conservatoire student I had studied the score of the *Oberon* overture, and the sweeping violin figures had incited my enthusiasm for the fiery, chivalrous nature of Weber. How great was my horror when, in a concert performance at that time, I heard next to nothing of those violin passages, only a meaningless *forte* on the D and A of the trumpets and kettle-drums which, in league with the *forte* of the trombones, drowned everything else. Occasionally, part of these passages emerged, only to disappear soon after, and the disturbed and disturbing impression of that performance—it was to be confirmed by other performances of classical works—at first called forth tormenting doubts in me, and subsequently made me realize that the clarity of melos must be defended by every means against these threats.

If, in view of life-long experience, my opinion were to be sought on the handling of brass and drums in classical music, I must issue a general warning against taking the direction *forte* below the notes in a material, dynamic sense. My advice is rather to give the *forte* the qualitative significance of *energy*, and besides, to treat it as a relative matter; i.e. never to ask for more vigour or brilliance from the brass than the musical meaning of the phrase in question permits or demands, thus insuring, first of all, that clarity of melos will be maintained. In most of those cases where the clearness of the thematic line or the distinctness of an important figuration is endangered by the natural notes of the brass in *forte*, the conductor will do well to moderate the latter to a still vigorous *mezzoforte*. Often, when an energetic accent is called for, it is advisable to make the brass enter *forte*, and to reduce it at once. I am, however, by no means advocating a consistent underplaying of brass and percussion in classical music: brilliance and vigour must prevail where they are demanded by the work, as long as the *forte* of those instruments is always maintained in the correct dynamic relation to the entire body of the orchestra.

Having spoken of my resolution to defend the clarity of melos against the encroachment of brass and kettle-drums *at all costs*, I may add that I have gradually learnt to consider only such means *legitimate* and conducive to my purpose as I found to be in accord with the character and style of the work, the intentions of the composer, or, more generally speaking, my reverence for the creative musician. Among such means I have often included well-judged general modifications of the dynamic directions. Here, it will often be advisable not only to curb the sonority of brass and kettle-drums, but to encourage the melodic instruments to special intensity of expression. For intensity is not only an emotional factor; its effect is also dynamic and thus conducive to distinctness. The actual acoustic supremacy of important voices over the others is not always sufficient for attaining complete distinctness of melos; the musician must be aware of the important fundamental difference between the quantitative-dynamic concept of *forte* and the qualitative one of *energy* (this is analogous to the distinction between the quantitative 'fast' and the qualitative 'fiery'). Thus, it is not merely through being played loudly, but through being played with energy and intensity, that a melody or passage will hold its own against the power of brass and kettle-drums or other dynamic counter-effects, such as, for instance, rapid figuration in other instruments which frequently endangers considerably the clarity of melos.

Apart from this *chief problem*, as I called it, the conductor is beset by various other dynamic worries, and he often has to admit to himself that a mere modification of dynamic directions is insufficient for achieving clarity of melos. In those cases, there is nothing for it but to alter the instrumentation itself if obscurity is to be avoided.

This brings me to the complex question of orchestral 'retouches', the conductor's active interference with the original instrumentation. Whatever can be adduced against this on the grounds of *literary fidelity*, I must declare myself against the radical rejection of retouching. As long as it is done solely in the service of clarity and faithfulness to the spirit of the work, and strictly for no other purpose, retouching may surely be counted among the legitimate means of interpretation. It goes without saying that the conductor has to refrain from interfering with the score as long as this is at all feasible; but if he cannot, by means of the given instrumentation, achieve clarity of dynamics or meaning, he may and should induce it by means of a (preferably small and unnoticeable) retouch; after all, faithfulness to the *letter* of the work should never obscure its spirit. But let us clearly distinguish between those alterations in the instrumentation that serve dynamic clarity or, in general, the clarification of the composer's intentions, and those arbitrary retouches that are used unscrupulously by some conductors as a means of musical interpretation. For example, I recall a concert performance of 'Wotan's Farewell and Fire-Magic' from Wagner's *Die Walküre* in which the conductor had the final chord played by divided strings. This was, apparently, more in accordance with his personal taste than the marvellous wind-combination of the original. He could not have doubted that an incomparable master of orchestration such as Wagner chose this wind-combination for the final chord of the 'Fire-Magic' out of a perfect inner realization of sound; still, to him, the conductor, the unmistakable intention of Wagner did not seem inviolable, and he arrogated to himself the right of substituting his own for it; in other words, he had no scruples in falsifying the sound of the Wagner orchestra.

Certainly, such crass cases of outrageous arbitrariness may be rare, but there is only a difference of degree, not of principle, between them and those rather frequent, less drastic, alterations of the score by which many conductors seek to *improve* or *modernize* the orchestration, believing themselves entitled to make changes in pursuance of their personal sound-ideals. I have seen scores of classical masterpieces where the notation had in places almost disappeared under the written-in retouches which arbitrarily adapted the original orchestration to the sound-ideals of another. But though his knowledge of the orchestra may be superior or his methods of orchestration more advanced, it can never be the conductor's affair to admix strange timbres to the proper colours of a score, to augment or change the character of, its sonority; in short, to subject it to his own taste by any sort of interference. Even the smallest licence in re-touching is to be deplored; yet, on the other hand, even incisive alterations, such as were recommended by Wagner in his suggestions about the performing of Beethoven's Ninth, may bear witness to exemplary re-creative faithfulness and be able, in a legitimate manner, to aid musical interpretation. In all reverence for Wagner and the exemplary purity of his intentions, however, I should like to say that his retouches here seem to go too far. But although I have my doubts about these radical alterations of Wagner, I am whole-heartedly in favour of the principle evinced by them of lending to the sound of the orchestra the fullest dynamic clarity, even if it is a clarity which could not have been obtained by the original orchestration. At any rate, I must enjoin conductors not to exceed the limits of absolute necessity when retouching an original score for the attainment of clarity, to keep the alterations as unobtrusive as possible, and to avoid under all circumstances even the semblance of external interference, let alone of an offence against style.

There, are, of course, scores in which great masters of orchestration, such as Berlioz or Strauss, Mahler or Debussy, have created all the instrumental pre-conditions for dynamic clarity. They have applied their profound knowledge of the orchestra and their aural imagination to the task of assuring the dynamic superiority of important voices by means of orchestration and by balancing groups of sound against one another; thus, they offer to the conductor on a *silver platter*, as it were, those means by which that fundamentally important acoustic clarity of orchestral playing can be achieved. In respect to dynamics, they give the conductor an easy task. Once he has gained from the thorough study of a masterly score an approximately distinctive inner sound-image—I say approximately, for even the *ablest* conductor will depend on actual sound for recognizing the aural intentions of the composer with the last degree of certainty—he will be in a position to arrive, with the help of extensive rehearsals, at a dynamically satisfactory orchestral performance. But the number of composers who think and feel orchestrally is not very large; there are not very many composers whose imagination is continuously fecundated by orchestral sound; who are so *at home* in its acoustic atmosphere that their musical ideas are born in orchestral garb, and composition and orchestration are an integral unit in the process of creation.

Most frequently, the conductor has to bring to life works which—usually dating from an earlier period—were primarily engendered by a purely musical imagination, as yet uncoloured by the realities of sounds—works very unlike those of the composers I have just mentioned, whose creation was influenced and accompanied by the orchestral sound images of the inner ear. Such works were first composed and later orchestrated, and usually the composer treated orchestration as a garment he had to weave on the loom of the orchestra in order to clothe his naked new-born child. But it does not happen very often in such cases that a vestment can be fashioned which will perfectly suit the body. Only where the profoundest knowledge and experience of the orchestra has been applied will it *fit like a glove*; only thus can a score be fashioned that wholly corresponds, in dynamics and tone-colour, to the musical content and character of the composition, lending clarity to the weave of the voices and creating, by expert use of orchestral devices, a sound-picture that is ruled by, and fully subservient to, the spirit of the work. Usually, in such cases, however, spirit and vestment do not entirely fit each other, and there remains a sort of hiatus between content and orchestral sound; the width of this hiatus naturally depends on how distinct the image of orchestral sound is that resides in the inner ear of the composer. If he possesses the capacity for the latter at all, together with a generally vivid acoustic imagination, then this hiatus will scarcely have a disturbing effect—and that despite the fact that the actual act of creation as well as the compositional work may not have produced concomitant orchestral sound images in him. Yet again, there are composers who are indifferent to this hiatus since they attach far less importance to the orchestral vestment, its colour and fit, than to the content. They pursue a sort of *factual* orchestration, and, provided they master the technique of orchestration to a sufficient degree, their scores can be made to yield sound-pictures which, though not interesting or attractive, are at least dynamically clear. In such a case, the conductor must, by means of a corresponding *factualness* in matters of sound that spells the latter's subordination to the purely musical aspect, adapt his performance to the intentions of the composer, as he attached far greater importance to the meaning of the composition than to the orchestral garment in which he clothed it.

All scores, then, that have been orchestrated by an expert hand can be realized by the conductor in dynamically clear sound-pictures. Where, however, the orchestral knowledge of the creator was insufficient, the conductor is faced by difficulties of interpretation which he cannot solve without the right mixture of faithfulness and boldness. There are scores which, as it were, resist live realization by the orchestra since they are written by an unskilled hand or have not sprung from the spirit of the orchestra; this is the case with Schumann's symphonic work. His aural imagination was predominantly under the sway of the pianoforte; he was not at home with the orchestra. Thus, an acoustically satisfying performance of one of his noble orchestral works will always be a serious interpretative problem to the conductor. Here, instrumental retouching becomes an unavoidable duty, for Schumann's original orchestration is unable to do justice either to the spiritual content of the work or to its thematic clarity, either to the spirit or to the letter.

In the chapter on the problems of balance in the orchestral ensemble a remark on the dynamic consequences of the bowing of string-players should not be missing. The conductor will soon come to recognize the drastic difference between the volume of a string-player's *forte* at the heel and at the tip of his bow; he will learn how tremendously the strength and intensity of sound can be enhanced by frequent changes of bow, and that the power of the strings will decrease in proportion as the phrases that are to be played on one bow become longer. He will find it advantageous to use down-bows of considerable length for achieving a perfect *morendo* down to the gentlest *pianissimo*; the latter is often attained by a light, rapid change of short bows at the tip. I should also like to mention the ethereal fineness and the special charm of the *tremolo* at the tip, and the floating sound of *cantabile* phrases in *piano* that are played only on the upper half of the bow. I cannot here enlarge on details of this kind, but I must point out the wealth of dynamic nuances—and therefore, of course, expressive nuances—that can be achieved by instructions or markings pertaining to bowing-technique. Their importance for the *soul* and *body* of string-sound, that is, for its expressive content as well as its dynamics—and, consequently, for the dynamic relation between the strings and other instruments—can hardly be overrated, and makes an intensive study of these numerous possibilities compulsory for the conductor. Mention must be made in this context of the decisive importance the various kinds of bowing and changes of bowing have for meaningful phrasing and expression. I for one have not ceased to this day to familiarize myself more and more with the general musical, expressive and dynamic consequences the bowing-technique of the strings has on the ensemble of the orchestra, and have tended incessantly to improve my instructions or directions on this point, in which endeavour I have been given new experience and insight by every orchestral rehearsal.

The different dynamic effects different proportions of strings to wind will have on the style and emotional demands of a work, and on the acoustics of the hall, must be given careful consideration. In general, it can be said that symphonic works written since Beethoven's time, and opera since Weber's, and the large concert-halls and opera-houses of our age too, demand a body of strings as large as it can possibly be made. All the same, in compositions like Ravel's *Le tombeau de Couperin* and Debussy's *L'après-midi d'un faune*, and in most works with a limited number of wind instruments, a reduction in the number of strings may be advisable in the interest of slenderness and clear transparency of sound; the same is sometimes indicated in compositions of quiet emotional character. Within the string-band, it is advisable to give special attention to the numerical relation of violins to 'cellos and basses. Mozart's basses should, with rare exceptions, sound slender, and, therefore, be small in number; in Haydn's symphonies, too, an impression of agility and lightness in the low register is usually desirable. In New York's Carnegie Hall with its three tiers and its capacity of about 3,000 listeners, I have often had good results in performances of Mozart and Haydn symphonies with a string-band of fourteen first, ten second violins, eight violas, six 'cellos and four double-basses; the same combination also satisfied me in my productions of *Don Giovanni, Figaro* and the *Magic Flute* at the Metropolitan Opera which seats about 4,000 listeners. Not even in the enormous Albert Hall of London did the same combination seem insufficient to me—on the other hand, I often preferred a yet smaller number of strings in smaller halls. For the earlier Mozart symphonies, such as the one in A major, the *Haffner*, or the *Prague*, for instance, a small number of strings is more appropriate than it would be for the last three; the *Entführung aus dem Serail* needs a smaller number of strings than *Don Giovanni*, and the *Requiem* in places demands a weighty string-sound. My advice, then, is take careful account, in making these decisions, of the acoustics of the hall as well as of style and character of the works.

For the opera conductor

The conductor's most complicated task in the concert-hall is, in a certain sense, a straightforward proposition when compared with the tasks he has in opera. For the stream of absolute music, notwithstanding its immeasurable musical content and wealth of expression, is a homogeneous element; thus, symphonic works set the conductor problems which, however intractable they may be, can be solved by means of purely musical endeavours. It is in this respect, then, that the integration and unity of his performances and their saturation with the power and quality of his ego offer no problem to the concert conductor.

It is otherwise with opera: it, too, demands of the conductor an effort of the ego, but this is here burdened with complications, for the 'I' is to make itself felt in conjunction with a 'thou', an 'it', and moreover, an abundance of other extraneous elements. The conductor shares the responsibility for all these elements, and if he fails to understand that a 'thou', namely the singer, has been allotted the position of protagonist in the art-form of opera, if he fails to allow him an adequate position in the interpretation as a whole; or again, if he conceives of the task of the opera conductor merely as a musician and not as an interpreter of the stage action, he will have missed the most essential point. And equally, he must incorporate in his musical aims the 'it' of the dramatic process; to wit, the spiritual atmosphere, the moods of nature, the ways of destiny, the external events of the action.

The fact is that the operatic stage is on a different artistic plane from the concert-platform: from Monteverdi and Gluck *via* Mozart, Verdi, Wagner, and Strauss to our day, the music of all stage works has been created so that musical expression is given to dramatic events and actions and their concomitant emotions, moods, situations, etc., and it is only by one's identification with its dramatic contents that one can and may interpret opera musically. Seeing that the singers are the carriers of the dramatic action—in other words, that the vocal parts give expression musically and textually to personal emotional impulses and external actions—the conductor has to provide for the corresponding spiritual and dynamic supremacy of the vocal side of the musical execution, and at the same time, for an orchestral approach that is instinct with dramatic significance.

If, in opera, he were to stress his own personality in the same dominating manner as in absolute music, this could only be at the expense of the individual contributions of the singers; that is, it would be to the detriment of the stage and thus the meaning of the drama which he should interpret *in its entirety*. There are opera performances in which dictatorship from the conductor's desk suppresses the artistic freedom and talent of the singers so powerfully that, instead of dramatic characters, pale shadows flit across the stage whose emotions and actions are unable to create the individual impression intended by the author. We also know—and this was specially common in former times—of dictatorship from the other side: the dictatorship of the singer who, unconcerned with the intentions and directions of the conductor, arrogates to himself all the rights of interpretation. In the case of those rare, inspired and fascinating singer-personalities whose intense dramatic and musical conviction forbids them to react to the intentions of others—personalities in whom something of the original meaning of the theatre manifests itself to excess; in their case and that of those who from conceit or ignorance ward off every suggestion of the conductor, we are dealing with forces which may do great damage to the interpretation, in that they distort the overall meaning of the art-work through overemphasizing an individual achievement on the stage. Lastly, one encounters opera performances—and that not infrequently—in which the conductor takes an interest in the music alone, and not in the stage: he conducts his orchestra and sees to it that the singers sing in time; but no bonds of feeling unite him to the stage; his impulses travel to the proscenium and no further; for him, the score, as the graphic sediment of an acoustic phenomenon, is all there is to the work; actions, characters, and situations remain outside his ken and do not have an influence on his music-making. But the look of an operatic score is deceiving: although, of the many lines that cover the page, only one or two are given to the singers, it is these that contain the intrinsic meaning of all that is written there in black and white; only the conductor who makes these lines his starting-point in a responsible approach to interpretation, will realize what the score demands of him.

The prerequisite for the profession of opera conductor, then, is an innate feeling for the theatre, a *dramatic nature*. Comprehensive and experienced musicianship must be augmented by a keen sensitivity to the vivid events on stage. The conductor must be able to identify himself with Iphigenia and Agamemnon; with Orpheus, Eurydice and Eros; with Cherubino and the Count; with Leporello and Elvira; with Wotan as well as with Brünnhilde and Fricka; with Tristan and Marke; and with Elektra and Clytemnaestra; deep in his heart, he must experience the loftiness of the Good Friday morning, the wildness of the scenes by the Valkyries' rock, the solemnity in Hans Sachs' workshop at the beginning of the third act of *Die Meistersinger*, the grief-laden fate of Amfortas, and so on— how else could he be a convincing interpreter of the music of these scenes? From this participation will grow his understanding for the individual tasks of the singers; it will enable him to be their adviser, to lend them that feeling of freedom which they need for giving an individual stamp to their roles, and yet to limit this freedom sufficiently for their stage-presences to be musically and emotionally compatible with one another and with the conductor's general interpretation. This is the manner in which his ego must manifest itself in opera: by authoritatively —or again, persuasively—encompassing all individual impersonations on the stage and all dramatic elements of the action, and integrating them in his unified musico-dramatic interpretation of the work. By this means he will integrate the great talent of a singer into his conception, put a stop to arbitrariness, instruct the inexperienced, and achieve unity of intention; and he will depend on his artistic gifts as well as on his ability to deal with people.

A deeper cause for the complicatedness of his task is the fact that opera does not represent so pure a type as a work of art as, for instance, the symphony. The combination of the visible and the audible, of word and music, action, and scenery and lighting —an interpenetration and continuity of elements which, though related, are yet heterogeneous—does not easily become a perfect organic unity. But perhaps it is just the problematic nature of this genre of art, its vacillating ambiguity, that explains its tremendous attraction for such creative spirits as Gluck, Mozart, Wagner, and Verdi, as also its centuries-old fascination for the widest audiences. As for myself, the problematic nature of opera has, during my life-long operatic career, been an ever renewed incitement to the finding of solutions—and beyond this, it has been a key for the understanding of imperfection as a magnificent challenge to the spiritual powers of man.

Opera resembles a winged beast of fable invested with the distinctive muse's head of drama and the fast-beating pinions of music. To mount, guide, and govern it, presents a strangely complex task to the conductor: he has to divide himself; his heart must beat with the orchestra, and at the same time pulsate in the stage action; he must proffer his own ego, but also that of every dramatic personage on the stage; he must dictate, and at the same time adapt himself.

This is not the place to discuss the relations between the conductor and the man responsible for the stage, the producer, whose spheres of work do, in fact, overlap. From the decisive importance of music for all that happens on the stage, it follows that it is the producer's duty to come to terms with the musical leader in all important matters as regards the stage. I shall return to this in a separate chapter.

But with respect to the purely musical part of the conductor's task, I should also mention that in opera, as in all vocal music with orchestra, the fundamental orchestral problem for the concert conductor of attaining clarity of sound and dynamic balance, becomes considerably more complicated. For here, once he has found orchestral balance, the conductor has to accommodate this to the vocal parts, the musical and expressive underscoring of which is one of his most important tasks. It will be clear from all the foregoing that regard for the voices in opera has a purpose that aims beyond intra-musical, dynamic purposes; it aims, to wit, at their dramatic significance. Mere *discretion* is out of place here; it is a matter of far greater import; the voices must be supported sympathetically by lively dynamics and dramatic expressiveness in the orchestra.

The opera conductor, however, has only been faced with

these dramatic problems since the growth in importance of the orchestral parts, largely due to Wagner. Originally, what the orchestra had to play, served mainly as an accompaniment and support to the voices; it assumed independent musical significance only in overtures, introductions, and interludes. Long before Wagner, to be sure, the importance of the orchestral element in opera had begun to grow. Composers loosened the tongue of the orchestra; the number of instruments, and their musical task and dynamic effect, increased with increased demands. Even in early Verdi the orchestral *forte* created serious difficulties for the conductor; with the increased numerical strength of the Wagner orchestra and, not least, the full symphonic role it assumed in music-drama, its dynamic relation to the vocal parts became a fundamental problem.

A glance at the score of *Tristan*, not to mention *Salome* and *Elektra* by Richard Strauss, will give one an idea of the difficulties one has to surmount in our day if one wishes to give the vocal parts their due, or rather their precedence, while preserving the symphonic status and expressive power of the orchestra. To tone down the orchestra without renouncing brilliance, weight, and clarity—this was the squaring of the circle that occupied my whole life; and my only regret is that I cannot express the results of my endeavours in the form of practical advice. But it is only his own experience and endeavours that can help the conductor in this province of his tasks; I must confine myself to pointing out once again that all that is essential in opera occurs on the stage, and that, though the conductor has to be a complete musician—no less than in the interpretation of absolute music—at the same time, his music-making must be instinct with those dramatic impulses that find their expression in the stage action.

CHAPTER IV

Music and Stage

Of the operatic theatre

The language that serves for daily—and everyday—intercourse between people, is also the *material* of the poet. But because of the manner in which he employs them the poet's inspired eloquence gives the same words deeper significance, more impressive beauty, greater elevation, in short, a tone of ideality; and that even when they are not grouped into verse. If, however, he goes further and heightens the expressiveness of his words and thoughts by the tonal and rhythmical values of verse-formation, he approaches the sphere of music. The plain man has no better way of praising a poem than by saying that it sounds to him *like music*. It is by virtue of this *musical quality* of metrical language that a verse-drama seems to be raised, whatever its content, to a sphere above reality, in which the emotions and actions of the stage are idealized and removed to some distance from actuality.

If, then, it is the *musical allegiance* of elevated and rhythmicized speech that gives ideality to verse-drama, music itself must have the same effect in even higher degree. For what is opera? A drama or a play that is sung and not spoken; that takes place entirely in the sphere of music; a drama whose events are clothed in music, permeated by music; whose acting characters express themselves in music. Not only does opera make no claim to reality—as an art-form it is divorced from it in essence and intention. Its world is even more *unreal* than that of the verse-drama in so far as it is lacking in that vestige of reality preserved by the verse-drama, the sound of the speaking voice.

Opera, then, belongs to a world above reality whose atmosphere is music. Not only does singing prevail in this world instead of speaking; and not only are all expressive possibilities of metrical speech greatly surpassed by the melodic content of singing; to this is added, by the orchestra, the eloquence of pure music which gives expression and support to all feelings, moods, and dramatic events enacted on the stage. In opera, the impact of dramatic events is enhanced through the use of music; music is able to make all stage action more moving, impressive, and dramatic. To write an opera means to create music out of drama, to put the power of music at the disposal of dramatic action. The composer puts his musical invention, his melodic-harmonic imagination, his symphonic skill, and the colourfulness of his orchestration, at the *service* of the dramatic action.

In no way, however, does Polyhymnia play a *subservient* part in the household of Thalia. Though music may have entered through the servants' door, it succeeded in unfolding its autonomous power—like a true *serva padrona*—wherever the opportunity offered. As soon as the poetic mood or the dramatic events of the scene ask for it, our art of music spreads her mighty wings, taking drama on her flight with her.

In other words: in those scenes that are loaded with emotion or filled with poetry, music takes the lead to such an extent that the climaxes of opera resemble a mighty torrent of music on which float dramatic elements, rather than a drama that is being given expressive power by music. The only examples I should like to mention here are the last part of the scene between Tristan and Isolde in the second act, and the end of the third act of the same work: in the surging billows of Wagner's music not only is *diurnal* actuality for the dramatic characters drowned; in the same flood, the visible world of the stage also dissolves for the listener. Scarcely less lofty are the crests of Mozart's gentler waves when they top dramatic events at the climaxes of his operas: Susanna's aria in the fourth act of *Figaro* seems to me another example for the fading-away of the scene under the overwhelming power of music. To be sure, Mozart's only wish was to express Susanna's feelings in that nocturnal scene: but the purely musical beauty of this immortal piece leaves any conceivable dramatic content far, far behind; its peaceful, noble melody against the floating orchestral background does not only speak of Susanna's heart; it also wields the innate magic of the beauty of absolute music; and no one whose soul is open to the pure element of music can fail to recognize that the world—even the world of the theatre—sinks away in the high floods of such music, and that the light of concrete experience is dimmed when the highest revelations of music take hold of our soul. Thus, drama itself finds a *Liebestod* in its affair of the heart with music. Its strongest emotional moments inspire the great operatic composer to a music in which they themselves are dissolved, by which they are *redeemed*. In the moving scene of Beethoven's *Fidelio*, when Leonora unlocks Florestan's chains, and soloists and chorus sing 'O Gott, welch' ein Augenblick' ('O God, what a moment is this') the dramatic action which gave rise to Beethoven's music pales away under the latter's power.

In contrast to such rare climatic moments when operatic music rises from the service of drama to be its ruler, there are passages where music undertakes the tasks of a more or less humble helper of the action or word. The so-called *secco* recitative allots to music its most humble role: here, opera differs from spoken drama only in that pitch and accentuation in the speech of the acting characters have been indicated by the composer. Between the two extremes—the overpowering of drama by music, and the emasculation of music by the drama —the character of their relationship changes incessantly. The mightier the emotional waves of tenderness, grief, passion, despair become, the higher becomes the importance of music in the general scheme of interpretation. The less the accent is on emotion in the events of the stage, the smaller must be the composer's musical contribution. A sober mood, factual statements, and ratiocinations cannot quicken his creative impulse, and it will be the word that takes the lead in such scenes, unless his creativeness were so outstandingly witty or masterful that it was able to emancipate itself from the strict service to the word and claim a significance of its own besides the scenic events. But whether music and action are of importance alternately or run their course in approximate equilibrium, dramatic elements will always—except in the above-mentioned extreme cases—exert a lively influence on the music, and music will always give expression to the stage action and support it by the force of its own expressiveness.

Above all: an opera is never a loose juxtaposition of two independent genres, but always a work of art of a particular character that has sprung from the organic conjunction and interpenetration of drama and music, and disposes of the powers of both components in accordance with the ever-changing form of their combination. Therefore, an opera libretto has no independent significance as a work of art, but is deliberately incomplete, being in need of music for its completion. Whether it is the expert product of an adroit librettist like Scribe, or the dramatic poem of a genius like Wagner, it is not designed as a play intended for performance, and it differs from the music-drama or opera based on it in the same way that the architect's blueprint differs from the house that is to be built according to it.

I recall that in former days it occurred not infrequently that an operatic producer directed his stage rehearsals with a textbook in his hand instead of a vocal score. Nothing could more certainly prove his lack of understanding for the art-form of opera. For he considered something partial—the text-book—as the entire work; what could result from this but a helpless performance in which the music, neglected as it was, and the producer's stage directions were at odds with each other? The orchestral preludes, interludes, and postludes, the scenic amplification and interpretation of which are an important part of his task would, of course, be missing from his libretto; but, in general, how could he dare, moreover, to base the form of a scenic event exclusively on the text, in ignorance or disregard of the meaning that is given by music to that scene? Or again, how was he to bring to scenic life, let us say, three minutes of music that was unknown to him, seeing that the few words that were set to it could be spoken in a few seconds? Thus the producer eventually had to realize it was necessary for him to satisfy the demands of music just as much as those of the book—he had to recognize that the peculiar and changeful combinations of musical drama in opera set him problems that were fundamentally different from those of the spoken play.

While the dramatic theatre, with its life-like, purposeful performing tradition—stemming from a great history—has long ago acquired the status of a serious cultural institution, the operatic stage was, until fairly recent times, given over to performances of a colourless routine that ill concealed an underlying utter perplexity and were injurious to the reputation of opera as an art-form. Who does not remember the primadonna, rooted to the spot in front of the prompt-box, hand on bosom, or arms outstretched; the singers who informed the public of what they should have said to their partners; the ensembles where soloists and chorus seemed to be frozen stiff, or rather, where the boards that are the world became a concert-platform for male and female singers in costume.

There are good historical reasons for the neglect of the histrionic side of opera, in contrast to the lavish care that was bestowed on the standard of singing. In most of the early musical works for the stage, the tragic or comic action was hardly more than a *pretext* for giving the singers an opportunity to render brilliant and effective vocal offerings. *Dramatic action* and what pertained to it was in the main allotted to the recitatives; acting did, in fact, occur there, but it was obvious that these recitatives were no more than connecting links between the formally rounded numbers, the arias, duets, trios and ensembles, the enjoyment of which was the avowed aim of those visiting the opera.

While, subsequently, dramatically gifted composers came to choose librettos that were able to call forth true human compassion, the style of performance in these works still remained within the former tradition though they had sprung from serious dramatic intentions, simply because its formal principle had not been subjected to change. For the division of opera into recitatives and *numbers* still held good; and although the latter served the progress of the action with increasing purpose, the decrepit but hard-dying tradition of opera-performance which considers the closed forms of even Mozart's and Gluck's operas as so many opportunities for vocal display, maintained itself for a long time. It was relatively late that artists and audiences developed an understanding for the fundamental difference in dramatic content between the works of these composers and those of earlier epochs; a difference that had long been hidden from view by the similarity of their forms. With the growing awareness that a new wine had flowed into the old bottles, endeavours towards a more adequate style of performance increased; but it took some considerable time before these effected definite changes in operatic production.

It was not until Wagner wrote his operas that a responsible style of operatic representation came into being. The demand for continuity in the dramatic interpretation of works and for polish in the individual acting had, in the first place, a beneficial effect on the Wagner performances staged by opera houses; but it gradually extended its influence over performances of works by the predecessors of the Bayreuth master. The inadequacy and lack of seriousness in customary performances of those older works could no longer prevail beside the higher methods of opera production which we owe to Wagner. To be sure, there first ensued a period of uncertainty, when a new style of performing the operas of Mozart, Weber, etc. was searched for; this style was no worse than that developed through Wagner's novel methods but it failed to apply these, as it should have done, to the *number form* of the older opera. It was left to Gustav Mahler, with his admirable insight into those works, to discover the inner law of their representation and to create, during the period of his directorship of the Vienna Opera, a new style of operatic interpretation, awakening to sublime life the works of Mozart, Gluck, Weber, Beethoven, etc. In all modesty, I may perhaps mention that during my directorship at Munich and subsequently at Berlin, my concern was to continue the reforms of Mahler; that is, to enlarge and intensify a serious method of performing opera.

When I was still young, I had already become aware of the discrepancy between the dramatic significance of operas and the performing tradition then prevalent. I well remember the dismal impression made on me by performances of Gluck's *Orpheus* or *Iphigénie*, Mozart's *Entführung aus dem Serail* or *Magic Flute*—the dramatic veracity and inspiritedness of these operas, their wealth of characters, even the intelligibility of their action, were suppressed by the dictates of a production whose dusty routine had never been touched by a breath of fresh air. What I soon perceived as a young musician was that the re-animation of the operatic scene could only proceed from the music itself; that the creation of a relevant style of opera production, therefore, could not be expected from a non-musician. And thus it happened in Vienna that a musician —and a musician of the highest calibre—set out to give shape to the proceedings on the stage in the spirit of music. Without Mahler's efforts, the operatic literature before Wagner might gradually have dropped out of the repertoire.

In all fairness, I must add that it was not only lack of understanding for the demands made by the music that was to blame for the helplessness of operatic producers before Mahler. The operatic producer, however gifted, has always suffered from the peremptory demand of opera-houses for their singers to be, first of all, *vocally* equal to their roles—I was very much aware of this during the long period of my operatic activities. While in the world of spoken drama acting talent and artistic personality are of decisive importance in engaging an actor, in opera, vocal capabilities used to be placed above all others; how often one was obliged to fill a role from purely vocal considerations with a singer who was unequal to its dramatic demands. In view of this irrevocable primacy of the voice, operatic producers, even today, have to contend with grave difficulties in their quest for an histrionically satisfying performance. Add to this the fact that vivid facial expression may impede technically correct tone-production, and that spirited acting may adversely affect the singer's breathing.

Singing and acting, then, often get in each other's way, and the former practice of having no action in 'numbers' and mainly reserving it for the recitatives was indicative of certain physical conditions; these the modern opera producer must not ignore, either; they are among the cliffs he has to circumnavigate. But whatever may be the disadvantages under which operatic acting, as distinct from straight acting, has to labour, these are amply counterbalanced by the dramatic expressiveness of the music itself, provided the producer and conductor succeed in exerting their influence over all the details of the performance.

The proliferation of external movement to be found in plays is generally lacking in opera; in the latter it is largely compensated for by the inner motion of the music. *From this follows the fundamental distinction between methods of dramatic production and methods of operatic production.* It would be wrong to apply to the supra-reality of musical drama the more realistic style of spoken drama—the two genres aim at essentially different goals.

But let no-one conclude from my reflections that individual acting is not of the greatest importance in opera, too. The times are past when the operatic public acquiesced in seeing all lovers, heroes, intriguers, sorceresses, and slaves suddenly forget their characters and relations to friend and foe, and

155

wholly engross themselves in their vocal problems. To be sure, even today one occasionally finds people who listen to the singing and the orchestra, lolling comfortably at the back of a box, and do not take the acting and its presentation very seriously. Their attitude is, as I have tried to show, historically conditioned: the decisive advance, instigated by Richard Wagner, in our concept of the opera-house, and its ensuing development from a place of vocal entertainment to a serious dramatic institution with singing performers and a vigorous approach to scenic matters, has by-passed these survivors from a former age.

For Wagner, however, and the generation educated by him, his music drama stands for the true beginning of a musico-dramatic art; this generation, though it conceded dramatic impulses to Mozart, Gluck, Weber, etc., saw these masters as nothing more than *forerunners* who had been prevented by the antiquated number-form from creating perfect works of art. Today, we see these masters in another light; paradoxically enough it is Wagner we must thank for this. As I have said, his work, teaching, and example brought about the development of a serious performing style on the operatic stage: its judicious application to the dissimilar demands of those older works has revealed that there pulsates in them a far richer dramatic life than a former manner of production would have one know.

It was then, in the light of such an interpretation, that the true greatness of those older operas was manifested. Mozart, Gluck, and Weber, stood revealed as the musical dramatists they were; they only needed an intelligent production of their works to prove their timeless vitality.

The difference in form between the older operas and those of Wagner and later composers does not, in my opinion, justify the drawing of a boundary-line between them, as was usual in former days. From the viewpoint of the producer who wishes to derive the principles of stage-presentation from the dramatic content of the music, Mozart and Gluck stand closer to Wagner than to their own contemporaries or predecessors.

For their music, too, has sprung from the spirit of drama, and therefore their works, although they contain 'numbers', must be performed as dramas.

On the other hand, however, I should like to advise the producer to examine carefully his idea of Wagner as a musical dramatist. The musician in Wagner often defies the radical maxims of the operatic reformer in him. While Wagner the operatic reformer theoretically declines the principle of closed musical numbers in favour of an uninterrupted flow of action, Wagner the musician infringes this self-imposed prohibition whenever musical inspiration fills him to the full. For, after all, what are Wolfram's 'Song to the Evening Star', Stolzing's 'Prize Songs', Siegmund's 'Love Songs', and even the trio of the Rhine-Maidens in *Götterdämmerung*, if not a kind of musical number which, in a manner not too unlike that of the old opera, stands out from the course of the action as a formally conceived vocal piece and dramatic resting-point? And, speaking quite generally, does not music spread its wings in Wagner's music dramas whenever the emotional excitement of the action demands it?

The time element in opera—problems of opera production

It is not only the passages of musical expansion that pose tasks to the opera producer such as are not encountered in the production of spoken drama. If a composer were entirely to forgo such musical expansiveness even in dramatic situations that allow for it; and even if he were to avoid, on principle, any musical eloquence in favour of the absolute supremacy of the action, there would still obtain a law to which the opera producer had to bow perpetually and unconditionally: it is that the tempo and duration of the music determine the tempo and duration of the scenic events. Whereas actors and play producers have a free hand, the stage-action of opera is governed inexorably by the time element of music. The duration of the music of a scene overrules any demands the producer may have as to the speed of its stage-action—he has to adapt his conception and his directions to the temporal consecution of the music; in this, the natural elasticity inherent in the shaping of any musical tempo will, of course, grant him a modest measure of freedom.

We touch here on one of the main problems of opera production, which accounts for its essential difference from the production of spoken drama: in the latter, it is the text, action, and dramatic appropriateness that determine the tempo of scenic events—in opera, it is music that dictates the tempo and duration of all details of performance.

In general, music proceeds more slowly—often very much more slowly—than would the action or the words without the music; thus the opera producer must usually extend the events on the stage in order to fit them to the music. This extension is in direct proportion to the autonomous significance of music as a language, or to its emotional intensity, and the producer is often faced with the following question: by what scenic action can I adequately fill the time that is taken up by this or that aria, ensemble, or outpouring of the composer's musical phantasy? The composer may have taken the liberty of musically extending a single dramatic moment to considerable duration; a duration that may be out of proportion to the dramatic significance of that moment within the progress of the action. Yet again, what is happening on the stage must certainly not divert attention from this dramatic moment even if it is being given, by music, a duration that is dramatically unjustifiable and thus, in a manner of speaking, puts a stop to the action.

There used to be current a very amusing parody of an Italian opera scene: someone has fallen into the water and is struggling for his life, while the chorus sings the words 'Quick, to his rescue!' with innumerable repeats ranging up and down its compass; any rescue action has to wait, of course, until this effective piece of music is over. Funny as this may seem, it is no more than a slight exaggeration of what we always experience in opera: namely, that the law of time in drama is not the same as that in music. The musical listener accepts this unresistingly, and nothing within him militates against the length of a revenge aria in which a baritone expresses, with considerable expenditure of voice, his fervent desire to stab his rival to death instantaneously, while being unable to take any action before the end of his musical offering. Nor is the listener's consent to this mysterious *timelessness* of music—for that is the quality in question here—restricted to works such as Verdi's *Il Trovatore* where, surely, no one has ever taken exception to Manrico's singing a *stretta*—and sometimes encoring it, too—before hurrying away to save his mother from the furious mob that is dragging her to the stake. Though it is usually less noticeable, every music drama and every opera is governed by this autonomous law of music— which may well be likened to the time-element of our dreams.

For our consciousness of time is 'benighted' by music. Just as we may dream of lengthy and involved events, only to find on awakening that we have slept barely three minutes, and a short dream may seem to fill a whole night, so music has the magic power of unhinging, as it were, the time-dimension of brief events, pressing situations, and momentary outbursts of emotion. In the *Arabian Nights*, we meet a tailor who, by the power of magic, keeps a man who is falling out of a window, suspended in mid-air until, having completed some urgent business, he is able to return and catch the falling man. Music is capable of exactly this: it can curb the urgency of dramatic situations, deflect the temporal demands of dramatic events into the realm of its dream-time, and subject the duration of dramatic events to its autonomous laws.

This, then, is one of the most essential tasks in opera production: to see that the scenic events, as they are laid down by the book, are adapted to the time-scale of music. As I have stated, the problem stems from the discrepancy between the effusiveness of the music and the sparseness of the stage-action; from this discrepancy can be deduced what I should like to call the 'attenuated continuity' of dramatic events on the operatic stage. We find here the reason why the operatic stage, however burning the passions, however violent the events that are enacted upon it, is a quieter sphere, all in all, than the stage of the playhouse, to which music's tendencies to expansion are foreign. If one is to avoid giving an impression of vacuity, let alone complete cessation of action, it can only be done by deriving a purposeful artistic style-principle from the above-mentioned 'attenuated continuity' of operatic action. In simpler terms: action on the operatic stage—dramatic climaxes apart—demands an unrealistic still-ness and breadth which, in conjunction with the dramatic vitality of music, will have the same natural and *legitimate* effect as the more concise, realistic tempo of the action of a play without music.

Without doubt, the production of the music dramas of Wagner or later works presents an easier task, in this respect at least; for Wagner and his successors made provision during the act of composing for a wealth of scenic details and their duration—let me instance the action of Sieglinde in the first act of *Die Walküre* before she leaves the hall—whereas the earlier masters were scarcely influenced at all, during compo-sition, by considerations of a scenic nature. All the same, the problem of the time-element does exist in music drama as well; by way of example I should like to mention that, in *Die Walküre*, the words of the parting Wotan to Brünnhilde, from 'Der Augen leuchtendes Paar' to 'so küsst er die Gottheit von dir', when spoken with the utmost intensity of feeling, occupy about seventy-five seconds, whereas Wagner's sublime musical setting fills approximately three minutes. No smaller is the difference in time between the spoken and sung words at Elektra's reunion with Orest in Strauss's powerful work. To whatever period, therefore, the musico-dramatic work may belong, provided that a true composer has been at work, the stage-action will always have to adapt itself to the laws of time peculiar to music.

But it is not only by way of expansion or compression of scenic events that the musical shape which a composer has given to a scene will affect its time-dimension. A single event, even a single gesture, must be adapted in duration, as well as in expression, of course—and more of this below—to the music. Every musically sensitive singer will strive, more or less unconsciously, to achieve external harmony between the rhythm of the music and that of the action: he will not often be tempted to carry out an energetic gesture demanded by the action without using an orchestral accent for it; for a change of facial expression he will almost always choose a moment where the mood of the music changes. It is one of the producer's tasks to show the singer the way in which the timing of his actions may be consciously adapted to the progress of the music.

In dancing, music gives the orders, and the dancer obeys. But it is only the rhythm of his movements that obeys the bidding of musical rhythm. The choreographic interpretation of melodic forms, on the other hand, does not obey this command, but artistically follows certain choreographic impulses that are derived from the music as a whole. As far as the relationship of music and dance is concerned, it is the former that sets the *tone*; and to this rhythm, body-movements, and expression, conform. In miming, to be sure, first place is taken by the stage-action; it was to illustrate this that the music was written; but even so, in actual performance the rhythm and expression of the music dominate the movements and the stage-action almost as much as the bodily movements of dancing.

Although in opera, too, we encounter the arts of dancing and miming in certain scenes—the third act of *Die Meistersinger* contains both—it is always live people that stand and act on the operatic stage, playing out amongst themselves scenes of great emotional import; in general, therefore, the relationship between music and action must never appear to be one in which the action is coerced by the music; we must be given the impression of co-ordination and harmony. Where, however, the composer intended his music to be illustrative, as for instance Mozart did in the unequivocal musical description of the fight between Don Giovanni and the Commendatore, or Wagner did in the scene of Beckmesser in Sachs's workshop, the production has to ensure exact synchronization between music and stage.

There are producers, however, who misunderstand this idea of creating the necessary harmony between music and stage; they strive for conspicuous synchronization of the kind described here, or for a precise mimic exposition of the music, even where the composer did not intend these. But to treat *illustratively* any music that was conceived spiritually and emotionally is to debase the *concept* of opera; if this is done, the concurrent stage-action will be given that admixture of mechanical elements which are an almost unavoidable feature of miming. Instead of this, I strongly advise producers to bring to the fore the psychological origin of every movement; even in the stage interpretation of pronouncedly illustrative music, such as Wagner wrote for the silent scene between Hunding, Sieglinde, and Siegmund in the first act of *Die Walküre*, and also for the Beckmesser scene in the cobbler's workshop, the execution, however precise it may be, must be preserved from assuming a machine-like character. If Beckmesser fails to slam the window exactly on the second crotchet of the bar that is intended for this, it would seem to me a lesser evil than if his gesture fails to show the rage that overcomes him at this moment. In short, not even in scenes that touch on the realm of miming must the mechanically exact correspondence between illustrative music and movement, desirable as it is, conceal the spontaneous psychological origin of the gesture. The salient point is that producers should do justice to the dramatic significance of music in the scenic events of opera, while still securing for them a semblance of unforced naturalness, such as is in keeping with the characters and emotions of the acting personages.

When Leonora says 'Wie kalt ist es in diesem unterirdischen

Gewölbe!' ('How cold it is in this underground vault!'),
Beethoven's music illustrates her shivering—but only the most
discreet suggestion of a trembling that is partly physical,
partly mental in origin, will accord with the dignity and seriousness of Beethoven's conception. The more convincing the
emotional quality of events on the operatic stage is to be, the
more care one must take to conceal the rhythmic correspondence of music and movement behind its psychological interpretation. An exemplary model of this is to be found in the
opening scene of *Die Walküre* between Siegmund and Sieglinde
with its passages of silent action. In Auber's *La muette de
Portici*, the actress playing Fenella has the difficult task of
keeping to the music with choreographic precision while her
acting is informed by the most heartfelt emotion. From
personal experience, I may relate that the dancer Grete
Wiesenthal—a most sensitive personality, of great musical as
well as choreographic talent—succeeded, in the production
of the work I directed at the Vienna Opera, in reconciling the
musical and rhythmical demands of the role with its dramatic,
emotional content; she expressed the latter most movingly.
To achieve this, to be sure, she had to do justice to choreographic exactness while treating the dramatic side of her task
as of prime importance. To achieve more drastic comic effects,
however, one may stress the rhythmically exact conver-
gence of music and gesture, even in opera. In my opinion, an
exact rhythmical correspondence is fully legitimate and desirable in cases where the action is accompanied by distinct
'visual' suggestions in the music, such as are provided by
Mozart in Susanna's aria in the second act of *Figaro*, during
which Cherubino is dressed up as a girl. Susanna orders him to
kneel down, rebukes him for his roving glances at the Countess,
and makes him get up and take some mincing steps. Mozart's
orchestra illustrated Cherubino's play very clearly indeed;
the singer is prompted, even, to put some variation into the
page's roving glances by the changes Mozart has worked into
the use of that charming motive. Although, in the scores of

these older works there are missing those verbal directions that were provided by Wagner and his successors for the stage interpretation of illustrative music, a musical producer will know how to shape such scenes so that they harmonize with the illustrative meaning of the music, while not robbing them of inner life by overemphasizing rhythmic precision or a certain approach to drastic comedy. The above-mentioned aria of Susanna is a touchstone for the sensitivity of producer and singer in the stage interpretation of scenic events contained in the music.

Zerlina's first aria in Mozart's *Don Giovanni* may serve as a further example: she begs Masetto to beat and maltreat her, but then to be friends again. Words and music give the singer an opportunity to depict graceful flattery, droll naïvety, and feminine seductiveness. The question must be asked whether the *fortuitous* employment of such expressive shades, provided it remained faithful to the text, would in itself do justice to Mozart's music, or whether the thematic material and the succession of musical ideas contain more definite scenic indications. To a true musicality, however, it will be abundantly clear that the graceful melodic turns of this aria call for cajoling movements or caresses, while bolder nuances of acting should correspond to the chains of trills in the violins.

If one excepts passages of such unequivocally illustrative force as the above-mentioned duel scene in Mozart's *Don Giovanni*, and those where the composer's express direction has related a musical phrase to a certain stage event, it still remains true that music never makes a definite demand for this or that gesture or action. Music merely contains scenic suggestions of a general kind; that is, it indicates the expressive realm within which the stage events have to remain; it demands, by a change in musical expression, a corresponding change in the emotional character of the action, and so on. If, however, this need for the general adaptation of the stage events to reflect the character of the music were to be ignored, it would become apparent that, *in case of conflict*, music would gain the upper hand. The expressive power of music is vastly superior to that of the stage; thus, in order to gain effectiveness, the stage action must accommodate itself to the musical meaning the composer has seen fit to provide.

As to the question of gestures, I might add that, although music does not prescribe definite movements—the composer must provide written directions if he wants these—a natural-looking correspondence between gestures and musical accents or rhythmical groupings is to be recommended. If a singer has to carry out an energetic action, such as falling to the ground, or some other dramatically significant movement, this should happen *with* the orchestral accent or rhythm rather than against it. In the night-scene of Verdi's *Un ballo in maschera*, Ricardo receives a solemn pledge from Renato: the sinister dramatic significance of the hand-clasp by which this is confirmed should be enhanced by the simultaneous, terrifying kettle-drum roll; otherwise, the scenic and the musical accents would contradict each other.

To sum up: a gentle gesture is incompatible with an energetic musical passage; and a lyrical musical phrase does not harmonize with an energetic movement; contrasts of this sort should be avoided as far as possible. Concentration and sensitivity are needed in judging whether the extent and character of the external action harmonizes with the music; the important question whether the music *gives its approbation* to the scenic events should be present in the producer's mind in all his dispositions.

Harmony between stage representation and music constitutes the highest law of opera production. Every offence against this, any act of negligence, must needs have an adverse effect on the dramatic events on the stage. By this harmony I mean something immeasurably more essential, profound, and *artistic* than mere extrinsic correspondence between orchestral and scenic sequences. It is the intrinsic approximation of moods and emotions on the stage to the emotional content of the music that must, above all, be the foremost concern of producer, conductor and singers. As a model for the combination of extrinsic and intrinsic 'musicalization' of the stage, I should like to mention the scenic tasks that have to be undertaken by Tristan and Isolde in the first act, after they have drunk what they believe to be a deadly potion. The external gestures and the psychological events are noted down verbally by Wagner and translated into music with the utmost clarity—however, the two performers cannot do justice to the dramatic demands of the scene unless they give themselves fully to the psychological transition described here, the transition from deathly defiance to loving ardour, and make their actions fit the orchestral description of this change of emotions. If the primacy of the emotional events were denied, the exact correspondence between gestures and music, albeit demanded by Wagner, would be empty and meaningless; and that in spite of the decisive dramatic significance that is held by this mute scene.

Apart from such exceptional cases of simultaneous 'extrinsic *and* intrinsic musicalization' of stage events, it is, in actual fact, the *intrinsic* harmony between stage event and music that determines the artistic significance and effect of an operatic performance. This harmony can only be achieved by the most intense empathy on the part of producer and singer with the dramatic meaning of the music. I should point out that in many cases no external movement or gesture is needed for creating harmony between representation and music: if, in *Figaro*, the singer of the Countess lets her heart be filled with the beauty of the orchestral prelude to her first aria; if her bearing is in accord with the pensiveness of this music, and she accompanies the changing patterns of the music with small changes in facial expression and posture, she will have acquitted herself of her task with far greater artistry and impressiveness than if she had employed those walks and changes of position with which a producer so often tries to 'fill in' the prelude. In general, I should advocate great economy of gesture and other body-movement, and I must stress once again that, because of the expressive power of music, it is in the nature of opera to demand less external movement than the spoken drama.

To avoid misunderstanding, I would say that music does not have a precision of expression that could command 'kneel down', 'clench the fist', 'slam the door'. But it is certainly able to convey humility, rising indignation, and the outbreak of anger, all of which may find their various expressions in scenic events. The actor-singer is committed to the dramatic emotional content of the music, though free in his choice of expressive means.

The producer's task of turning the stream of music onto the wheels of his dramatic mill is, however, less problematic than it would appear to be. The dramatic content of operatic music is, after all, quite well known to him in a general way; for this music was in the first place inspired by the same scenic events which he has to represent; it will depend on the degree of his musical sensitivity whether his directions remain in accord with the music not only as regards the total character of his stage interpretation but also in its details.

There are *idiosyncratic, interesting,* and *inventive* productions in which not only the music, but even the original significance of the drama have been ignored by the producer. Nothing easier than to achieve sensational stage successes by entirely unfounded *innovations*; by the introduction of ideas that have nothing to do with the work. But however talented and stage-worthy such ideas may be, however sensational the success of such *neologisms,* their lack of *authenticity* dooms them to failure in the near or distant future. Only the production which takes account of the basic dramatic intention behind the scenic event, and its musical setting, will give an authentic impression. Besides, music is capable of fighting back. The dramatic significance which it lends to the stage events triumphs effortlessly over inapposite audacities in the production by rendering them ineffective.

I would like here to quote again Nietzsche's saying from *The Birth of Tragedy from the Spirit of Music*: 'Music scatters the sparks of images'; that means to say, the art of music, whose realm lies beyond that of the visible world, has the power of calling forth visions in the listener. To be sure, these mysterious emanations of music are of a nature too vague, fleeting, and changeful to give rise to definite indications as to the shape of scenic events. And yet—to the true stage talent and to a true musical sensibility—these image-associations will lend valuable support; they will stimulate the theatrical imagination and save it from errors.

It is true that the relationship between music and the visible cannot be understood or defined with complete clarity; yet the real artist will be *instinctively* aware of harmony or disharmony between music and the shapes and colours of what appears on the stage. Regarding the decorative aspect and lighting of the scene, too, we are bound to recognize an extrinsic and intrinsic relation between music and stage. Music controls the change of scene from the Venusberg to the purlieus of the Wartburg in *Tannhäuser*; it controls the moonrise at the end of the second act of *Die Meistersinger*, the flashes of lightning during the battle of Hunding and Siegmund, as well as those in the fourth act of *Rigoletto*. But more important than this unproblematic conformation of the stage events to the music is the 'musicalization' of the stage in those cases where music should exert its intrinsic influence on the tragic mood of a stage event, as for instance in the annunciation of Siegmund's death in *Die Walküre*, or in the ghostly atmosphere of the graveyard-scene in *Don Giovanni*, or in the dewy morning-scene at the beginning of the second finale in the *Magic Flute*. Here, stage-lighting with its many uses becomes an effective ally of music; this alliance is less problematic than any other kind of combination between the audible and visible sphere of the operatic theatre, yet at the same time it is of great importance for the desired 'musicalization' of scenic events. An exemplary model for this is found at the beginning of the third act of *Tristan und Isolde*; the despondency of the orchestral introduction, the playing of the shepherd's pipe, and the total emotional atmosphere of this scene, can combine to profound and significant effect with the forms and colours of the dilapidated castle, the view of the sea, and the character of the lighting. And how impressive can the right combination of landscape and light and music be, in the 'Elysian Fields' of Gluck's *Orpheus!* The producer has no better way of serving the stage representation of opera than by deriving his inspiration from the music, both for creating the drama and for establishing the work's visual ambit. The sensationalism of productions that strive for novelty at all costs, will falsify them, however inventive they are; again, a work may wither away under the sober factualness of an over-simplified production; as I have indicated here, it is only the 'musicalization' of the stage that will give to the works performed their fully legitimate and lasting effect, and grant flourishing life to the operatic stage.

CHAPTER V

Notes on Bach's *St. Matthew Passion*

In my autobiography, *Theme and Variations*, I have recounted with what feelings of repentance I used to remember my annual Easter performances of the *St. Matthew Passion* during the ten years of my activities at Munich: owing to the great demands made on my time and energies by my operatic duties, I had taken over the cuts customary in the local performances of this work, and despite persistent misgivings, retained them. It was not until twenty years later that the long-desired opportunity offered itself of making amends for my shortcomings: I succeeded in giving an uncut performance in the series of New York Philharmonic concerts. This time, I was able to find time for thorough preparation. It was possible for me to reassess my view of the many problems that the work presents to the interpreter, and I renewed my study of the rather voluminous literature dealing with the interpretation of Bach in general, and of the *St. Matthew Passion* in particular. As the result of this extensive preparation and the thorough rehearsals undertaken, a performance took shape for which I felt I could, as far as this is at all possible, bear full artistic and moral responsibility. I had decided to perform the work in English so that the words in conjunction with the music should make an immediate emotional impression on the listeners; here is the place to express my lasting gratitude to the meritorious translator of the text, Dr. Henry S. Drinker. His rendering of the German text into English showed great linguistic aptitude and a real understanding of the music; it was an essential contribution to the profound impression made by this and subsequent performances of the work.

I discovered the significance of numerous problems of detail in the course of my studies; one decisive result they had consisted in a realization made but imperfectly during my Munich period: that of the irreducible totality of Bach's creation, the inviolability of its form, and the damage that must needs accrue to the latter from any excisions.

The literature surrounding the *St. Matthew Passion* is so exhaustive and voluminous that it seems unnecessary for me to set forth here a detailed account of the insights I gained from my studies, and the rehearsals and performances. It may not be amiss, however, to recount here some quite personal thoughts and experiences, the result of my labours of those days, which may perhaps prove to be a helpful supplement to the general literature on the subject.

The general plan of the work

Before occupying myself with detailed questions of interpretation, I have always found it useful to arrive at an idea of the general plan of a work I am to perform; to become aware of the spiritual atmosphere from which it grew, of its structure, of the relation of its parts to the whole, etc. The realizations gained from these endeavours indicate to me both a fundamental concept of, and the detailed approach to, the work's execution. This is how I proceeded in the case of the *St. Matthew Passion*, and I should like to preserve in this book some of the results of my endeavours and of the light shed thereby on the work's interpretation.

The work contains a trinity of groups, each belonging to its proper sphere; a trinity which is held together by the forming hand of Bach in a powerful unity. The first group comprises the protagonists of the action that takes place in Chapters 26 and 27 of the *Gospel according to St. Matthew*. To the second group belong the pious individuals and the choruses connected with them that accompany the action with their emotions and comments. The third group is the Christian community whose chorales appear, within the animated profusion of action and sentiment, as the pillars that carry the edifice of the work.

Schematically, then, we have to imagine three regions: the first is the real, terrestrial region of the historical events, containing the localities at which these events take place, such as the palace of the High Priest, the house of Simon the leper, the coenaculum, the Mount of Olives, the place Gethsemane, the hill of Golgotha, the sepulchre. In this space move, speak, and act the figures of the Gospel: Jesus, Judas, Peter, the High Priest, Pilate, Pilate's wife, the witnesses, the women, the soldiers and their captain, the disciples, the priests and scribes, and the people. To their sphere belongs the evangelist Matthew who is narrating their actions and sayings.

The second region is a spiritual one. Thence come to us the voices of the pious personages who in their recitatives and arias express their profound participation in the sayings, conduct, and fate of Jesus. These soulful figures correspond, as it were, to the figures of the devout and prayerful, in their relation to the Saviour, or to the Holy Family in medieval paintings. From the same, supra-mundane dimension issues the gigantic *chorale-fantasia* of the beginning, 'Come, ye daughters, share my mourning.'[1] These are, in Picander's text, 'the faithful and the daughter of Zion', experiencing, and accompanying with their plaint, the Saviour's journey to Golgotha. By virtue of the power and profound emotional strength of Bach's polyphonic flood, however, this *chorale-fantasia* becomes a world-encompassing dirge and self-accusation by mankind, overlaid by the solemn angelic chorale of boys' voices 'O Saviour, meek and lowly'. I feel this piece to be a vocal introduction which, not unlike Beethoven's third *Leonora* overture, uplifts the essence of the subsequent drama into the realm of

---

[1] This and further translations are those of Ivor Atkins, in Elgar's revision of the work, Novello and Co., London.

music, thus preparing the souls of the listeners for the imminent dramatic events. To the same supra-mundane sphere belongs the duet of the two women who mourn the imprisonment of Jesus, and are interrupted by the anguished choral outbursts 'Loose Him! leave Him! bind Him not!', and followed by the desperate invocation of hell's fury upon the head of the betrayer. The *chorale-fantasia* at the end of the first part, 'O man, thy grievous sin bemoan' falls into the same category. In its verbal content and emotional tone it is a touching reflection on the life of Jesus from birth to crucifixion; being placed, in the work, after the seizing of Jesus, it interrupts the progress of the historical events that proceed on the plane of reality. Thus, the two opposite *chorale-fantasias* enclose, like two heavenward columns, the earthly scene of the first part in which the drama of the Passion up to the kiss of Judas and Christ's imprisonment is played out. The recitatives and arias of this section pertain for the most part to the inward realm of the soul, constituting a meditative, lyrical contrast to the dramatic events of reality which grow out of them and are to reach their climax in the second part. They, in turn, are followed at the close of the work by the solemn, consolatory epilogue which comes from those transcendental regions—by the pious souls' thanksgiving and valediction to the Saviour, and the chorus 'In tears of grief, dear Lord, we leave Thee'.

Common to these two groups—that of the figures of the Gospel and that of the compassionate witnesses—is their manifest contemporaneity with the historical events of the Christ drama in the first century, and therefore with the beginnings of Christianity. The chorales, on the other hand, occupy a third, more distant plane, a timeless *afterwards*— in them, we hear the voice of developed, existing Christianity. The protestant congregation, its singing idealized in noble four-part writing, calmly and confidently sends its solacing message down the ages into the time-bound, changeful, anxious world of early Christianity the evangelist tells us of.

As we know from Spitta, Picander, the author of the text,

had his words printed and re-printed with the omission not only of the biblical text but also of that of the chorales. His authorship, therefore, is restricted to the words of the meditating, sympathizing, confessing figures of our second, supramundane region. Again, it is clear from Spitta's classical biography that Bach exerted a decisive influence on the work of the pious but not highly gifted Picander. Considering the profound emotional and musical significance of those sections of the work, these facts reveal to our eyes a moving aspect of Bach's own heart; in the emotional power and devotion of those sections, there shines forth the personal Christian faith of the creative musician. It is, moreover, due to Bach's decisive co-operation in the making of the text that the rich variety of those meditative songs fits in so purposefully and harmoniously with the words and actions of the historical Holy Week, and also with the liturgical sound of the chorales.

Questions of interpretation

I was once asked by a young musician whether Bach should be performed in a romantic manner. The question did not refer to that romanticism which fills the music of Schumann or Weber, the poetry of Novalis, Eichendorff, or E. T. A. Hoffmann. The questioner had in mind a vividly emotionalized interpretation—impermissible in his view—which had none of that academic exactness and 'objectivity' which for him constituted the proper Bach style. My answer to the question—the only possible one, I think—was: let us follow our hearts, and put into our performances of Bach's music the same intensity and truthfulness of feeling that we meet on its every page. What I have said in the chapter 'Of expression'—namely, that no music exists for which an expressionless style is suitable—is of course true for the entire output of Bach, from pieces such as the *Inventions* for clavier to the great vocal works. But we must of course realize that the manner and degree of expressiveness in our music-making has to be derived from a reverent approach to, and intimate knowledge of, the spiritual content of Bach's compositions. From my own endeavours in this direction I have learnt that Bach's works, with all their diversity and an intensity of expression that embraces the mightiest emotions, have as their basis an exalted calmness. Bach's secure faith united him to a higher world—it is only an instinctive recognition of this allegiance that will provide us with the key to his music. Excesses of temperament, brilliance, and virtuosity, and frequent changes of dynamics or expressive nuance will, therefore, be out of place in the re-creation of an art that presupposes a state of inner calm in the performer as well as in the listener.

Certainly, wherever Bach becomes a dramatist, as for instance in his characterization of the real acting and speaking figures, he demands an unstinting vitality of expression—from the goodness, the solemnity, and the sorrow in Christ's sayings to the penitent despair of Judas before the priests, and the furious outbursts of the people. The performers of such sharply etched figures as Peter, Caiaphas, Pilate, etc., must show by their lively delivery that they are at all times aware of the dramatic significance of their parts; I should even venture to state that the dramatic claims of the actual Passion events must take precedence, in case of doubt, over the fundamental calmness of Bach's spirit. The evangelist, to be sure, is not one of the acting personages—he tells a story; but he tells it with a sense of intense participation, exemplified by the delivery of such passages as 'And he went out, and wept bitterly'; a similar treatment is indicated for his entire *recitativo* narration. To those who advocate an 'objective' narrator's tone for the evangelist I should like to point out that Bach had in mind the inspired apostolic soul of Matthew when writing these recitatives.

Bach, in his role of dramatist, then, does not speak with his own voice; the voices we hear are those of the actual participants in the Passion drama. We do, however, hear his own voice and perceive his own heart in the singing of those pious, compassionate figures of the work's second dimension. The singers of those arias and recitatives must find the right delivery by immersing themselves in the piety that inspired Bach in the writing of these sections. In this sphere, any individualizing dramatic characterization is out of place—the singers are nameless—and yet, Bach's *faithful heart* has filled these supra-mundane figures with the pure, warm life-blood of his music, thus personifying them on their own, lofty plane. Expressiveness in these sections will therefore aim at a state of rapt absorption; yet however great the intensity of feeling, in general, a noble sense of proportion must prevail. A word of warning should be given to the soprano and contralto: let them bear in mind that Bach wrote their parts for boys' voices; neither the sentiments of mature womanliness nor a luxuriant tone of voice are apposite to their task.

From my advocacy of moderation, however, the chorus following on Jesus' capture, 'Have lightnings and thunder their fury forgotten?' must be exempted. Here, the spirit of the drama has penetrated the supernatural realm of the soul, and only the full impact of violent expression can do justice to this piece. But sometimes we are faced with a sort of *muted* drama in the spiritual sphere: an imaginary *scene* in this region reflects, as it were, the real scene of the Passion drama. I am thinking in this context of the tenor solo 'O grief! that bows the Saviour's troubled heart!' and the subsequent 'vigil' with its soft chorus entries—it is as if the fateful events of Gethsemane were continued in a similar nocturnal scene within the spiritual realm of those participating souls. It is from the mysteriously dramatic character of this scene that the mode of expression used by the soloists and chorus must arise.

The inward lyricism of the recitatives and arias of this second group reaches its peak in the sombre mood of the women's duet 'Behold, my Saviour now is taken, moon and stars have for grief the night forsaken'—the intermittent flashes of the anguished cries in the chorus only serve to make the nocturnal scene yet blacker.

QUESTIONS OF INTERPRETATION

The beginning of the second part, too, brings an imaginary dramatic event: Zion seeks Jesus, bewailing the loss of the friend, and the faithful grieve with her, offering their help and speaking lovingly to her in the words of Solomon's *Song of Songs*. Our imagination is offered the image of the 'fairest among women', surrounded in her search by compassionate, ministering figures; it is from this agitated image of a tenderly erotic character—probably unique in Bach's output—that the interpretation has to take its stimulus for the emotional and musical execution.

Among the scenes within the supra-mundane realm of the participants I also count the bass aria 'Give, O give me back my Lord'. Its bold, peremptory character sets it apart from the general tone of the arias in this sphere, and I have always felt as if the release of the captive Saviour were here being demanded by the very man who had drawn his sword and smitten off the ear of the High Priest's servant. Among the arias that put an imaginary scenic occurrence before us is also 'Come, healing Cross'—we see here the figure of Simon of Cyrene who takes the cross from the faltering Saviour. The alto recitative 'O gracious God' gives rise to a shattering vision, too—that of Christ's scourging. In other songs of this group, however, it is only a state of the soul that finds expression, as in the recitative 'To all men Jesus good hath done' and the subsequent aria 'For love my Saviour now is dying'. I have long felt the latter to be one of the most exalted compositions of Bach: the arch of its melody is sustained by the purest strength of love, and the immaterial, floating orchestral sound of the solo flute with the two oboi da caccia—without bass or organ—contributes to the impression that this aria is, as it were, an angelic message from the sphere of the Holy Grail.

The right delivery of the chorales follows from their function within the plan of the work. In them—as I said above—the voice of the timeless Christian community intercepts, in solemn anticipation, the historical events of its origin. From

177

Bach's chorales we learn of the judgment pronounced in the realm of eternity on the temporal, human events of the first century. This specific, anachronistic significance of the chorale in the course of the work must be made clear by the performance. Let me instance the chorale ' 'Tis I, whose sin now binds Thee' which, to all appearances, belongs to the scene between Jesus and the disciples, for it provides to the eleven-fold perplexed question 'Lord, is it I?' the answer ' 'Tis I', which therefore should be sung by the disciples. But it is Jesus Himself who—after the chorale—answers the disciples' question by saying 'he that dippeth his hand with me in the dish, the same shall betray me'. The disciples' question and Jesus' answer are separated by the chorale; that is to say, the ideal community interrupts the progress of the action by a truly Christian confession of sinfulness and guilt. After this interruption, which removes us from the historical course of events into the realm of timelessness, we return to the scene of the Last Supper. Another example is afforded by the chorale 'O Sacred Head, surrounded by crown of piercing thorn'. Who are they that sing this? The evangelist tells that the soldiers spit on Jesus and smote His head with the reed, and we know of the people's hostility. It can only be the timeless community of Christians, living and deceased, proclaiming across time and space the compassion and ardent love of Christ that inform this chorale; it is the visible and invisible church together from whose region issues this exalted song of fellowship that uplifts the shattered participants in the story of Christ's Passion.

The realization of the specific position of the chorales has come to me not only from my study of the *St. Matthew Passion* —my study of the work only went to corroborate the experiences I had during my own performances. In Munich I was already asking myself why every entry of a chorale shook me to the roots of my being. The answer which I found, and in which I was confirmed by the renewal of these experiences in New York, has been vouchsafed to me in the form of an intuition, almost indescribable verbally. Nothing but this lofty concept will describe what happened to me: with the entry of the chorale, cosmic expansion was gained by that which I had previously had to re-create out of my own emotional resources as a historically and locally confined dramatic scene. What came over me was beyond the sphere of drama and beyond the feelings of the participating faithful—in the words and in the solemn pace of the chorale I perceived mankind united, dedicated, confessing, praying; every time, I was aware of a harsh change when we returned from the world-embracing sphere of the chorale to the confined space of the Passion drama. I never think, therefore, of the chorales as part of the drama, even when their words, called up from the distant past, as it were, seem to refer to the utterances of acting persons or the evangelist.

As to the execution of the chorales, I should like to remark that, being songs of fellowship, they will suffer from individual expression, emotional dynamic changes, and tempo variations. A model not to be disregarded is the chorale singing of the congregation in church, which is innocent of dynamic gradings and freedom of tempo and comes to a halt on the pauses, expecting the organ to renew the impulse for common continuation. Since in Bach's chorales, however, artistic four-part writing is substituted for the primitive unison singing of church congregations, it seems to me that a corresponding *stylization* of dynamics and expression is permissible, and even indicated: I would not have had the chorale 'O Sacred Head, surrounded by crown of piercing thorn' sung otherwise than with the greatest solemnity and full power, or the chorale 'Be near me, Lord, when dying' otherwise than softly and with profound inwardness; besides, I knew I was in agreement with tradition in this. The execution of the chorales, therefore, should always be adapted in sentiment and dynamics to the content of the text, while the same dynamic level should be maintained from beginning to end. If this is done, I think it will be possible to do justice to the spirit of a song of fellowship that has been raised to the sphere of ideality.

Why some musicians should feel impelled to ignore the *fermate* prescribed by Bach at the verse-endings of the chorales, is a mystery to me. Since I have been criticized for my own fidelity to these *fermate*, I should like to point out that those pauses are traditionally observed in church to this day—they must always have served as a *meeting-point* after the unavoidable divergencies in the unison singing of the many. Moreover, Bach has not prescribed these pauses in the chorales alone; he has *written them out* in the *chorale-fantasias* at the beginning and end of the first part, by setting extra voices against the basic chorales.

Liberties

We can no longer be guided by the number of executants that were under Bach's direction in St. Thomas's Church, Leipzig; we must make allowance for the musical and emotional requirements of the work and the acoustic properties of our large concert-halls or churches. The sound of the opening *chorale-fantasia* must give an impression of billowing fullness if Bach's intention is to be preserved, and there must be a good leavening of boys' voices if the chorale is to hold its own. The number of executants must be large enough to be equal to the dynamic demands of this gigantic composition in the place where it is performed. Yet I must warn against the employment of the massed choirs that are sometimes used in performances of Handel's *Messiah*. If the numbers of singers were in excess of what is demanded by the *chorale-fantasia*, the chorus, 'Have lightnings and thunder their fury forgotten?', or the hostile outbursts against Jesus in the second part, the result would be an excessively material kind of fullness, injurious to the stern severity of Bach's idiom. Some suitable reduction of vocal forces is to be recommended for the double chorus of high priests and scribes, 'Not upon the feast', or the disapprobatory remark of the disciples, 'To what purpose is this waste?' The number of singers must be carefully adjusted to the lovingly reverent expression of the disciples' question, 'Where wilt thou that we prepare for thee to eat the Passover?' This passage, as well as that of the mortified question of the disciples, 'Lord, is it I?' was set by Bach for four-part mixed chorus, and I am convinced that his choir did sing these two passages chorally, and included sopranos and altos, although there are only twelve—male—questioners, and eleven in the second passage. Eleven times the question is put, 'Lord, is it I?'— Judas does not take part, and it is only after the chorale that he asks 'Master, is it I?'; in my opinion, these passages should also be rendered chorally, though with a small number of singers; a conductor with a sense for the dramatic meaning of these two passages will avoid the full choral sound and, by dynamic grading and quantitative restriction, strive for that dramatic truthfulness which—to say it again—I recognize as Bach's most essential demand for the rendering of the events of the Passion story. All the mightier, then, will be the entry of the full chorus in "Tis I whose sin now binds Thee', which reveals the dominating significance of the chorale in the organism of the work. Similarly, the moderate number of those who in the palace speak to Peter and those who answer to Judas's self-accusation, 'But what is that to us?' should be distinguished, by numerical reduction, from the massed enemies of Jesus in the savage double-choruses, which should have greater dramatic weight. The fanatical outcry, 'Barabbas', manifests a dramatic boldness and dynamic vigour in Bach's invention such as the choral resources of his day certainly could not have afforded him. Despite my principle of reducing the number of singers according to the scenic action, I have felt compelled— against the words of the Gospel—to summon up all available forces in one particular passage. The evangelist tells of the uproar of the elements, the opening of the graves after the death of the Saviour, and says, 'Now . . . the captain and they that were with him . . . feared greatly, saying "Truly this was the Son of God" '. 'The captain and they that were with him': this can only mean a small number of people; but I thought it right to have those bars sung by both choirs with the utmost abandon, with full accompaniment of orchestra and organ. For Bach's gigantic setting of these words must be understood as an avowal made on behalf of all mankind, of the belief that Christ is the Son of God, and I could not doubt that all that have tongues should join in this avowal.

Concerning the number of strings employed, we may feel quite independent of Bach's Leipzig orchestra. It is clear that the body of strings must be adequate to the demands of the first *chorale-fantasia* and the chorus, 'Have lightnings and thunder their fury forgotten?', and that it must be adapted, as a matter of principle, to the acoustic properties of the place of performance. A few desks will be sufficient to produce the tender, celestial tone imagined by Bach's inner ear, which in the accompaniment to the words of Jesus should surround His person like a halo. For the semiquavers at 'I will smite the shepherd, and the sheep of the flock shall be scattered abroad', on the other hand, I recommend the full complement of strings, which should then be retained to the end of the recitative. There are a number of similar passages where a sudden increase in the number of strings will swell the shimmering tone surrounding the words of Jesus to full orchestral force; in the Saviour's reply to the High Priest, for instance, 'Nevertheless I say unto you, hereafter shall ye see the Son of Man. . . .' The importance of the orchestral contribution grows here in proportion to that of the words, and therefore its sonority must increase, too. A very full body of strings is demanded, in my opinion, by the passage in which Jesus institutes the Eucharist. This is not at all a case of those tenderly gleaming string harmonies by which the recitatives of the Saviour are usually distinguished from those of all other persons. Here the orchestra has full musical significance, and this I always strove to underline in my performances, preserving, of course, the proper relationship between voice and accompaniment. Moreover, the organ should give its solemn support here to the sound of the string orchestra.

This brings me to the thorny problem of the continuo. We know that Bach in his performances always used the organ as a continuo instrument in all recitatives, arias, choruses, and chorales. Notwithstanding my endeavours to be faithful to Bach's intentions, I found myself unable to follow his example in this. An organ played continuously for five hours would be a source of fatigue fatal to the receptivity of the listener, even if there were the most varied registration. The ear, which under the impact of ever-enhanced combinations of sound since Bach's time has become a more refined, more perfected organ; and the psyche and the nerves, which in over two hundred years have evolved an increased sensitivity, an augmented need for variety, no longer possess the steadfastness and rest-fulness of that earlier cultural epoch. In so extended a period, a period in which momentous historical and cultural events have exerted their influence on humanity, it was unavoidable that a new way of listening and a different kind of musical audience should come into being. I am aware that I am moving onto unsafe ground with these assertions, and that I cannot really prove anything by them. No amount of uncertainty in my reasoning, however, could dispel the certain aversion of my ear and musical sense to the uninterrupted sound of the organ throughout the entire work. If I had been a musician of the epoch comprising the end of the seventeenth and the beginning of the eighteenth century, such persistence of sound might well not have irritated me at all. However, inured from my youth to the orchestral sound of our time, I was con-scious of having to pay regard, in my performances, to the development in our musical perception and receptivity, not-withstanding my fidelity to Bach. I was greatly encouraged in this attitude by finding in the book of the eminent Bach connois-seur, Anna Gertrud Huber, *On the spiritual paths of Johann Sebastian Bach and Ludwig van Beethoven*[1] a laudatory mention of an essay by Arnold Schering which contains this remark:

[1] *Auf den Geisteswegen von Johann Sebastian Bach und Ludwig van Beethoven*, Beiträge zu einer Renaissance ihrer Werke, etc., Strasbourg, 1938.

'Assuming a work of Bach were to be performed in its original garb, as it were, and with absolute stylistic correctness—let us imagine a Leipzig performance of 1724—would it elicit in the modern listener the same impression in all its subtle proliferations as in a listener of a hundred and eighty years ago? Obviously not. In the meantime, a new capacity for discrimination has been instilled into our ear and musical receptivity by countless masterpieces of the past century. Our store of musical experiences contains impressions from Haydn, Mozart, Beethoven, Weber, Chopin, Schumann, Brahms, Liszt, Wagner, and others; impressions which have so fully become our own that we can no longer discard them'. This essay is of the year 1904; meanwhile, even ampler worlds of sound have opened up; was it not desirable, then, nay imperative, for me to take into account the new attitude towards listening in my realization of Bach's score?

The following deviations from Bach's own manner of performance are, in my opinion, justifiable: I gave the chord accompaniments in the recitatives of the evangelist and of the figures of the Passion drama with the exception of the Saviour, to the harpsichord, with a 'cello and a double-bass strengthening the bass-line. The harpsichord was also given the harmonies in passages such as those of the false witnesses and the two priests; in addition, the continuo in 'impious' choruses, as for instance, 'Not upon the feast', or, 'To what purpose is this waste?' and in all choruses of Jesus' enemies, too, the continuo was executed by the harpsichord. For the recitatives, arias, and choruses of our 'second region', however, and equally, of course, for all chorales, only the organ was considered. In the registration of the organ accompaniments everything possible was done to achieve a sensitive adaptation, in dynamics and timbre, to the musical and emotional content of the sections thus accompanied—I had in mind how Bach, the master of the organ, might improvisingly have used all the resources of the instrument for this task.

Furthermore, I endeavoured to give dynamic vitality to the

orchestral playing; to free it from the rigidity into which many a musician is betrayed by the lack of dynamic markings—apart from the summary *forte* or *piano*. In the melodic structures of Bach, there lies for every feeling musician a live dynamic flow that can be translated into sound within those often very extended *forte* or *piano* stretches prescribed by Bach. But my earnest advice is to preserve in this 'vitalization' that inner tranquillity which is the hallmark of Bach's faithful soul, as it is, to some degree, of his commitment to his age. The unrest of *modern* dynamic variegation has to be eschewed for serious stylistic reasons—and not only from *historical* considerations. Further, the use of the oboe for long stretches in many parts of the work—as for instance in the bass aria, 'Make thee clean, my heart, from sin'—was to my feeling incompatible with our tonal susceptibilities, and I took the liberty of mitigating its monotonous effect by a *tacet* at places that seemed to me suitable. In some of the chorales where Bach puts the oboes with the sopranos throughout, I thought fit to relieve them from this, in the long run, tiring sound; among others, in the chorale after the death of Jesus, 'Be near me, Lord, when dying'. But I did not feel justified in having the latter sung *a cappella*, as is often done—like all the other chorales, this is intended as a song of fellowship and would lose its character if sung *a cappella*.

The question of the *da capo* in the arias weighed on my conscience for a long time. Important considerations of form impressed upon me the necessity for obeying the direction; and I am to this day distressed by the thought that I did not do this but contented myself with the repeat, not of the whole main part, but of the *ritonello*; however, I at least achieved by this a close in the tonic key of the aria. In short, it was in this manner and by other measures which it does not seem necessary to expound here, that I attempted in my performances to take account of the difference between our form of listening and that of Bach's time as far as was compatible with my reverence not only for the spirit but also for the letter of the work;

and I believe that I can bear the responsibility for what I did.

A view of ornamentation

The voluminous literature on the subject of ornamentation is confusing and frequently contradictory. Having zealously studied the authorities and pondered the subject for many years, I have arrived at the decision to be led henceforth entirely by my own feeling in the execution of ornaments. For I have not succeeded in becoming so much at home in the world of the grace notes and symbols that I have the assurance of an expert in their execution. But I do believe that I have found the reason for these profuse embellishments: the composer feels that a simple musical texture should be *spiced*, as it were, by the insertion of fleeting dissonant elements. From the rule that an *appoggiatura* should enter on the beat on which the main note to which it belongs is placed, and that the latter should then be shortened according to the duration of the former, it is apparent that the point of accenting a dissonant note lies in a nuance of harmonic progression. Philipp Emanuel Bach writes in his *Essay on the true art of playing Keyboard Instruments*[1]: 'The *appoggiatura* alters the chord which without it would be too simple' —that is to say, the fleeting dissonance should give savour to what without it would sound too plain. The rule of starting the trill on the upper note has the same purpose. But ornaments serve as a condiment not only for the harmonies, but for the melodies, too—these trills, *appoggiature*, *acciaccature*, mordents, etc., enliven a musical texture which otherwise might be too plain, giving it nuances in accordance with the taste of that cultural period. An extensive era of music-making stood under the sign of the art of the grace-note, as was established by Adolf Beyschlag in his *Ornamentation*[2]. The influence of

[1] *Versuch über die wahre Art, das Klavier zu spielen*; 1753, 1762. (English translation by W. J. Mitchell, New York, 1948.)
[2] *Die Ornamentik der Musik*; Berlin, 1908.

ornaments on the direction taken by the musical taste of that age reminds me—if such an extravagant comparison will pass muster—of the influence the discovery of the Spice Islands had on the refinement of the palate.

I should now venture the unprovable and certainly disputable suggestion that the sapidity of the ornaments makes its effect not only on the harmonic and melodic, but also on the rhythmic, plane; and that this is particularly so in the case of the *appoggiatura*. The notation of this ornament preserves the element of liberty: the fact that an *appoggiatura* may be noted as a quaver or a semiquaver by no means determines its actual length. Even the scholars of ornamentation leave open the question whether, for instance, the *appoggiature* in the violin-solo of the aria, 'Have mercy, Lord, on me',

Ex. 8

should be played as semiquavers,

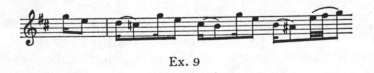

Ex. 9

or as quavers.

Ex. 10

As a second example I choose the theme of the women's duet, 'Behold my Saviour now is taken',

Ex.11

in order to express a thought which my study of ornaments has called forth in me: is it not just the inexactness or unclearness in the notation of the value of an *appoggiatura* that gives us the key to its meaning and execution? I have come to the conclusion that the *appoggiatura* was not intended to be a crotchet, quaver, or semiquaver, i.e. a rhythmically exact subdivision of the melodic structure, but rather an indefinite and indefinable time-value which was to carry an element of unrest or indecision into the rhythmic plan, thus providing a rhythmic stimulant. So that ornamentation would seem to fulfil its function of inducing sapidity in all three component aspects of music—melody, harmony, and rhythm. Since I discovered this, I have always treated the ornaments of older music accordingly, and I have experienced no disappointment. But I am quite aware that I am not on the safe ground of incontrovertible logic in this matter; I thought, however, that I should mention this idea of mine in a report on what I endeavoured to do in the *St. Matthew Passion*.

It remains for me to speak of the great significance contained, in my opinion, in the contralto aria, 'See the Saviour's outstretched hands!' Does not Bach here step outside the plan of the work that he laid down in collaboration with Picander? I consider it likely that the piece only came into existence during the course of Bach's work, which at first covered chapters twenty-six and twenty-seven of the Gospel alone. The events begin on Maundy Thursday and end on Easter Saturday—that is, they extend from the Last Supper to the sepulture of Jesus, the work finding its solemnly mournful conclusion in the mighty chorus, 'In tears of grief, dear Lord, we leave Thee'. Though some of the Saviour's recitatives contain intimations of His future Resurrection, the twenty-eighth chapter of the Gospel, in which the angel tells the women of the Resurrection and it is related that they, and later the disciples, encountered the resurrected Jesus, found no place in the *St. Matthew Passion*. The sepulture is followed merely by the benediction and thanksgiving of the four pious characters and the final chorus I have mentioned. Our aria, then, is nothing less than an anticipation of the Resurrection; it is the only section of the work that deals with the events of Easter Sunday. Its words and music radiant with the light of beatification, it allows us to partake in the vision of a soul that directs the glances of its fellows to where its own are aiming: to the resurrected One. The long spun-out, hovering 'See ye' of the beginning is already instinct with blissfulness, for the seer perceives the figure of Jesus transfigured as He is holding out His hand to help those who seek Him. How could her words relate to Him whose hands are nailed to the cross? She calls 'Come!', the chorus asks 'Come where?', and she answers 'In Jesus' bosom seek redemption, seek ye mercy'. She calls 'Seek them!', the chorus asks 'Where?', and she answers 'Live ye, die ye, rest ye here, ye whom sin and guilt oppress, rest ye in Jesus' bosom'. The words alone make it clear that the permanent refuge promised by her to the lost sinners cannot be in the arms of Him who is dying at the cross. It can only be the outspread arms of Christ resurrected, prophetically seen by the speaker, that offer this haven to the sinner. However, any doubt that may still be entertained after a consideration of the text must vanish before the blissfulness of the music. Its floating sound is an immediate answer to the recitative, 'Ah Golgotha, unhappy Golgotha!'; it dispels the latter's affliction by an intimation of the events of Easter Sunday.

Finally, a word about the mysterious turn taken in its last bar by the chorale, 'Be near me, Lord, when dying'. To my knowledge, this is the only instance of Bach ending a chorale with a modulation instead of the tonic chord as is customary in congregational singing. The modulation leads from the C major of the chorale to the tonic chord of the submediant, and this E major surely conveys no sense of finality, but rather of premonition and expectation. In this departure from the chorale's basic character—it is almost a disruption—Bach seems, to my mind, to point to the mystery of death as of a transition, a new beginning. The moving significance of this mysterious passage calls to mind the words of St. Paul in the first letter to the Corinthians: 'We shall not all sleep, but we shall all be changed'.[1]

The greatness of Bach's *St. Matthew Passion* can only be measured by those who recognize in this sublime masterpiece the apostolic inspiration that brought it into being.

[1] *I Corinthians*, XV, 51.

CHAPTER VI

The Mozart of the *Magic Flute*

On the occasion of January 27th, 1956

The thought of the imminent celebration of the bicentenary of Mozart's birth has brought home to me my obligation to acknowledge, for once in writing, the genius whom, as a musician, I have endeavoured to serve all my life. Above all, this must be an expression of gratitude for the sublime happiness with which the creativeness of Mozart has illumined, has blessed, my life. To state in detail the reasons for this feeling of gratitude, that is, to advert to the beauty and significance of the works with penetrating thoughts and words—this seemed to me superfluous in view of the copious, and for the most part excellent, literature on Mozart; nor could I hope thus to serve Mozart better than by my efforts in the opera-house and concert-hall. I do believe, however, that on this festive occasion I should touch verbally upon a phenomenon on which that otherwise so plenteous literature sheds no light, but which seems to me most worthy of attention and has for long increasingly engaged my interest. It is that while there is today perhaps no other composer whose work is as generally loved and familiar to the world as Mozart's, his personality has remained strangely obscure to the world. From the biographies, from musicological and historical essays, from reports, letters, and anecdotes, we learn a good deal about his works, and their genesis and significance, and about the external course of his life; we learn about what he said and did, but the personality all this conjures up can only be aligned with difficulty with our knowledge of the creative genius as it manifests itself in the greatness, the seriousness, and the overflowing wealth of his works.

Beethoven's human personality stands clearly before our eyes; it impresses us decisively as that of a world-conqueror in the realm of the spirit. In his tearing-up of the *Eroica's* dedication to Napoleon we recognize the same tempestuous force that informs his musical idiom, and the *Heiligenstädter Testament* seems to us like a Beethoven Adagio in words; nearly everything, in fact, that is known to us of his personal character and conduct—his human relationships, his letters, the reports of his friends, the conversation-books, his profound wish for self-improvement—all these show his mighty, inspired, Promethean soul, instinct with all that is sublime as it speaks to us with overwhelming expressive power in his music.

In the case of Richard Wagner, his writings form an inexhaustible source of information about his thoughts and feelings. From his Beethoven essay, to take only one example, there emanates an all-embracing humanity such as must be assumed to be the generating force behind his gigantic life-work. In his letters to Mathilde Wesendonck one feels the power of love of the heart that has given to the world the unique and undying miracle of *Tristan*. And the historic deed of creating the Bayreuth Festival fittingly complements the coherent aspect of a nature conceived on the grand scale.

On the other hand, what do we know of the human personality of Wolfgang Amadeus Mozart? His letters show a sincere, lively, decent character, an open, trustful soul; he appears in them as a loving, obedient son, a devout Catholic, an affectionate husband, and so on—as a musician, too, who ponders the problems of his art and is fully aware of his genius—and most frequently, as a carefree, fun-loving young Salzburgian. But it is neither in these personal documents nor in the reports of contemporaries, nor in words and actions of Mozart that have come down to us, that we can discern the master of immortal symphonies and operas, and the dramatist whose creative phantasy gave figures and scenes buoyant with life to the theatre; nothing we know of Mozart the man could render credible to us the creator who with the shattering voice of the Stony Guest invokes eternity; who, his soul sensitively attuned, found in his music the ironical, and yet benignly understanding tone for the amorous entanglements of *Così fan Tutte*; who in the coloraturas of the Queen of the Night conjured up the vision of the sparkling starry night-sky; who in the lofty message of Sarastro expressed the deepest love of mankind.

A similar disparity between human personality and artistic greatness might be found by some in the case of Bruckner, whose character, yet more naïve, not to say primitive, than Mozart's, seems to stand in a similar mysterious relation to the power and significance of his creativeness. I for one, however, cannot find this a cogent comparison: Bruckner was an absolute musician, and his great soul was not in need of an abundance of worldly experience, intellectual life, and literary culture for him to be able to write his mighty symphonies with their transcendental content; these sprang from the impulses given to his elemental musical creativeness by the boundless emotional resources and exalted visions of his soul. And as regards his vocal compositions and masses, the words and meaning of these sacred pieces offered no problem to his pious, dogmatically devout heart.

Mozart, however, was by disposition and inclination a musical dramatist, and no dramatic creativeness is possible without a penetrating understanding of the inscrutable human heart, of every kind of relationship between people, and of the peculiarities of cultural conditions; that is to say, without wide experience of the world and knowledge of men, without a good many intellectual interests, without comprehensive culture.

To be sure, this concept of the dramatist is not directly applicable to the dramatic musician who by his music intensifies and *de-realizes* the actions and the inner life of figures that come to him in a libretto written by another. But the figures of Mozart's libretti were often originally no more than shadowy outlines, and it was his imagination and dramatic vision which gave them, by means of his musical power of exposition, their life-blood, their clear contours, their definite character. Thus, we are right in recognizing in the musical characterization of stage events and of acting personages such as the servile intriguer Basilio, the plump Osmin, the pert and crafty Pedrillo, Leporello and Masetto, Despina and Dorabella, Monostatos and Papageno, the true dramatist in Mozart whose figures have become clearly defined beings, and even close familiars to us.

As we shall scarcely succeed in building a bridge from the simple though infinitely lovable personality we find in Mozart literature to the miracles of such creativeness, the attempt to build a bridge in the opposite direction remains to be made; we must look to his works for enlightenment on the true spiritual stature of Mozart.

It seems to me that we may be guided in this undertaking by the realization of a unique fundamental trait in Mozart's creativeness which manifests itself in two forms both of which point to the same source: truthfulness becomes beauty, complexity becomes clarity; every musical characterization of people, sentiments, moods, and events in Mozart's stage-works becomes transported, without loss of truthfulness and conviction, to a sphere of exalted beauty; the most vivid diversity of dramatic events is moulded into the perfect musical form. It is this beauty and perfection of form which allows us to look deeply into Mozart's being; we may conclude from it that his heart was filled by some transcendental harmony which exerted a decisive influence on his artistry. Everything he created, his dramatic and vocal works as well as his absolute music—the latter even at moments where strong expression is given to discordant emotions—is nurtured by this supra-mundane sphere and maintains the overtones of a *transcendental* consonance. Sensing this inspiration that reigns in Mozart's soul, we may well speak of a seraphic impulse giving wings to his musicianship and his music. And I beg leave here to make the personal confession that the sublime happiness which my contact with Mozart's creation has brought me, is felt by me to proceed from that consonance which is resoundingly proclaimed by his musical world.

While from Beethoven's work there often issues the fire and the might of a prophet, and Bruckner's work seems to tell of the inner world of a saint, it is an angelic sphere that reveals itself in the beauty and perfection of Mozart's music, in its exalted range of serenity and purity. This pervasive supramundane element in Mozart's nature may even go to explain that sensation of remoteness which so strangely and mysteriously enters our image of a personality with whose artistic creations we are well acquainted. Perhaps it may even account for Mozart's profound understanding of human character and emotions—an understanding not in need of the varied experiences of more mundane natures. It is certainly doubtful whether Mozart was conscious of that higher nature of his that was the driving force behind his music and is manifested in it. What he became fully conscious of, however, in the later years of his short life was the growing accord of his love-filled heart with the Masonic tenets of humanity and brotherliness. From the synthesis of the former—and most probably unconscious—impulse with the latter moral tendencies there arose the spiritual sphere that found artistic expression in the *Magic Flute*.

Thus I believe that in this immortal opera, his last, we may come close to Mozart himself and perceive his first personal avowal, if not indeed the only one that allows us fully to look into the depth of his heart. As Shakespeare, after remaining all his life the anonymous dramatist concealed behind the figures of his stage-works, at last appears before our eyes in the person of Prospero in the *Tempest*, so, I think, we at last encounter in the *Magic Flute* the human personality of Mozart himself.

To be sure, the original form of the book would not have

made this encounter possible. The fairy-play, based on a tale of Wieland, which Schikaneder fashioned into a libretto for Mozart, is altogether lacking in those ethical motives which in the ultimate version determine the plot and the course of the action decisively. The book contains picaresque events, fantastic figures, and comic and serious scenes of the kind which Schikaneder, the experienced man of the theatre, could have presumed would, in conjunction with Mozart's music, bring him a great theatrical success. He had designed the role of Papageno for himself, and we may therefore assume that he had intended the comic scenes to be the dominating part of the action. We do not know exactly and can only guess how much Mozart had to do with the alterations that resulted in the definitive form of the text-book. I suppose Mozart was able, in the first place, to induce Schikaneder to introduce Masonic ideas, because the latter was, like Mozart, a member of the Masonic Order. It must have been in connection with this, then, that the most incisive alteration was made, that of the figure of Sarastro who had originally been conceived by Schikaneder as an evil sorcerer, but had now to appear as a sage and noble leader of the priestly community. The fact that the introduction of high ethical ideals in the person of Sarastro was due to Mozart's demands is proven by the obscurities in the action which resulted from this change in the central figure; the skilful Schikaneder would surely have avoided them if the alterations had proceeded from his own initiative. As it is, one is puzzled and disturbed to find the wicked Monostatos in the service of Sarastro and appointed prison-warder of the gentle Pamina by him. Though the most conspicuous, this is not the only obscurity of the book, and we may conclude from these weaknesses that Schikaneder's artistic conscience was not on a level with his flair for effective stage-events. However this may be, we must concede that, in spite of the irritating inconsistency of the action, the libretto not only has theatrical vitality but also contains serious and significant features, and poetical felicities which have retained their impact to this day. No better testimonial to its merits could be adduced than the pleasure which Goethe had from it; it gave him the idea of a continuation under the title *The Magic Flute, Part Two*. The approval that was bestowed on the book by such a great artist is quite understandable, for the *Magic Flute* with its fanciful extravagance and its mixture of childish mirth and serious solemnity fulfils to an astonishing degree the requirements that the author of *Faust* puts into the mouth of the theatre-director and the comic actor in the *Prelude upon the stage*. It may be assumed that it was Schikaneder who contributed the adventures and the merriment, and Mozart the solemnity—and some of the fun. The message of loving-kindness, forgiveness, friendship, and a promised 'better land', however, gained through Mozart's music so uplifting and convincing a power that the Sarastro scenes became, surely very much against Schikaneder's original intentions, the main action of the play. In the music of these scenes we hear the beat of Mozart's heart and we cannot doubt that in creating the figure of Sarastro he wished to portray his ideal of humanity.

With the transformation of Schikaneder's sinister Sarastro into Mozart's luminous figure—a lofty, hieratic proclaimer of loving-kindness—the youth Tamino and his quest for admittance to Sarastro's realm were bound to acquire a correspondingly high significance. If, in creating the figure of Sarastro, Mozart acquaints us with his ideas of human greatness, wisdom, and godliness, then in Tamino, who is so irresistibly drawn to the world of Sarastro that he is willing to undergo any trial to gain admittance to it, can be seen Mozart himself and his ardent striving for ideal humanity. His love for Pamina—the erstwhile motive of his errand—merges, after his discourse with the Speaker, with the yearning for initiation into that world. Pamina, to whom the thought of losing Tamino's love means death, who unhesitatingly goes through fire and water for him, represents his feminine ideal. And Papageno, the cheerful fellow, the simple son of Nature who likes to eat well and hankers after pretty girls—who is he? What does his continual companionship in the progress of an action that speaks so eloquently of Mozart's own being mean? Well, he accompanies Tamino everywhere because he too is Wolfgang Amadeus Mozart, he too belongs to Mozart's being. For in Mozart's breast, as in Faust's, there lived two souls. He was the high-minded seeker, filled like Tamino with the ideals of exalted humanity. At the same time, he was a cheerful, good-natured young man whose mind was bent on worldly pleasures. And as in the *Magic Flute*, the Tamino in Mozart's soul always had the better of Papageno and rebuked him for his frailties; yet again, on occasion, the latter showed himself recalcitrant in face of the former's moral admonitions, and we may assume that the struggle between the two souls, though never very violent, was everlasting. But we also know that his companionship with Papageno did not prevent our Tamino from pursuing the 'path of virtue' resolutely through all perils and trials until the goal of his journey, his admittance to the sun-temple, was achieved. On the other hand, it was in vain that Mozart searched for a Pamina such as was granted to Tamino. His earthly pilgrimage did not bring him the ideal life-partner whose image lived within him. However, Mozart's belief in the ideas of Freemasonry find their convincing expression in Tamino's determination to undertake the arduous journey, and in its victorious completion.

It remains for me to draw attention briefly to the musical style of the work and its difference from the master's earlier operas. Never before had there been anything in Mozart's music like the combination of C minor *fugato* and the chorale of the 'Two Men in Armour'. The solemnity of the overture, the grotesquely comical wildness of Monostatos' aria, the lofty enthusiasm of Tamino's monologue before Pamina's image, the scintillating ornaments of the Queen of the Night, the overflowing brotherly love in Sarastro's E major aria, the mystical invocation of Isis and Osiris by the chorus of Priests—all these are new in-spirations of Mozart's genius, new colours on his palette. With the exception of the overture and the above-mentioned fugue, however, the *Magic Flute* shows a pronounced simplification of orchestral language in comparison with earlier works. It is the simplicity of highest maturity, as is also evinced, for example, by Wagner's *Parsifal* in comparison with his earlier music-dramas; the absolute inevitability with which this style brings Mozart's genius to its point of highest mastery, tells us something very important about Mozart's individuality.

I am, however, aware of only one personal statement of Mozart's that points towards those depths of his soul which are witnessed by his music. This exception to the usually so worldly tone of his numerous letters is contained in a communication of the thirty-one-year-old Mozart to his father:

'As death is, strictly speaking, the true end and aim of our lives, I have for the last few years made myself so well acquainted with this true, best friend of mankind that his image no longer terrifies, but calms and consoles me. And I thank God for giving me the opportunity of learning to look upon death as the key which unlocks the gate of true bliss. I never lie down to rest without thinking that, young as I am, before the dawn of another day I may be no more; and yet nobody who knows me would call me morose and discontented. For this blessing I thank my creator every day, and wish from my heart that I could share it with all my fellow-men.'

So he thought of death every day, 'in blissfulness'; this fully shows how close to eternity his heart was; it shows the unearthly harmony in it which informs his music as a seraphic sound. For the rest, however, this most communicative, not to say talkative, of men was silent about those depths of his soul of which he himself may for long periods of time have been only vaguely conscious. Only the *Magic Flute* unsealed his lips, and there he laid bare his heart—in Sarastro's and Tamino's words and strains; and in the former's pronouncements, the world should recognize Mozart's own spiritual testament. Yet though Tamino's striving was gloriously crowned in the end, Mozart was glorified only *sub specie aeterni*—long after his troubled earthly life had found its sad end. Yet even in this wearisome earthly pilgrimage we may discern a wondrous analogy with the errand of his hero in the *Magic Flute*. As to Tamino, the 'good gods' had granted to Mozart the protection of sound against the dangers besetting his path: the music that accompanied him on his life's journey gave him the courage, the noble serenity, and the vigour of soul which no adverse experience, no poverty, worry, or illness, could take from him.

And just as the melodies of Tamino's flute prove their protective magic even in flames of fire and floods of water and their blessing descends on Pamina and Papageno, too, so to this day—and today perhaps more than ever—Mozart's music proves its beneficent, helpful, enchanting power with everyone to whom it speaks.

CHAPTER VII

Retrospect and Prospect

My work on the present book, which now draws to a close, has occupied me—though with frequent and prolonged interruptions—for more than eight years. The mood it was begun in—one of tranquil contemplation and of a serenity in keeping with my age—was not destined to last. I confess that this mood became increasingly tinged with a feeling of sorrow, even sadness; for the further the book progressed, the larger loomed the harassing question whether the thoughts, opinions, and counsels that are foregathered in this 'testament' of a musician do not belong to the past—together with the musician who through them essayed to give expression to an essential part of his life's artistic harvest. More and more it seemed to me as if the conflagrations whose smoke darkened the first half of the twentieth century, also signified a twilight of the gods in the realm of the spirit that had been my homeland. What else could have induced and intensified in me that feeling of strangeness which I experienced in the atmosphere of public music-making, so familiar formerly? Had the shrines at which I had prayed and sacrificed all my life really fallen into decay? Is the lofty source of all great art, creative inspiration, in abeyance, and is it a declared *anachronism*, to be replaced by laboratory methods based on abstract principles, applied experimentally, and producing art for the satisfaction of intellectual interests? Yes, it does indeed look as if materialism and intellectualism have taken hold of the present generation, and allotted to the arts a lower place in the life of society than the exalted sphere in which they have hitherto reigned. On that lower plane, however, there scarcely exists any distinction in rank between art and ordinary entertainment; they live next door to one another; and instead of festively raising themselves up to art from every-day life, or being lifted out of it by art, it is possible for people today to make a neighbourly call on it, quite at their pleasure and without any spiritual commitment or heightening of the emotions. For me, however, and surely for all who worship art in the hitherto accepted manner, it is exactly the elevation of our souls which we seek and find in art, and which Schiller had in mind when in *The partition of the earth*[1] he makes Zeus say to the poet: 'If thou wilt dwell with me in heaven, as often as thou comest, thou shalt be admitted'. Should one not fear for a generation in whose vocabulary the word 'elevation' will soon have an exclusively aeronautical meaning, perhaps; a generation which expects from a work of art not a heart-moving experience, but only entertainment, stimulation of intellectual interests, or even the satisfaction of an inherent sensationalism.

We may be helped in understanding the meaning and extent of this change in the mental outlook of our epoch if we turn our attention to a topical phenomenon whose contemporaneity with the decadent trends of our culture seems to point to a causal nexus: I am referring to the superabundance of *entertaining matter*, and in particular, to the facilitations and amenities that are extended to the everyday consumption of cultural values— these, running parallel to similar achievements on the plane of our material existence, have resulted in a marked decline in the effort made by the individual. Great as our appreciation must be for the fundamental improvement in our material circumstances which we owe in large measure to the astonishing advance of technique, we are liable to have misgivings about the ease with which anybody can participate nowadays in

---

[1] *Die Teilung der Erde*: 'Willst du in meinem Himmel mit mir leben, so oft du kommst, er soll dir offen sein'.

numerous artistic and scientific attainments without having to take the trouble of working for them. Let us consider how superficial a culture must be which is disseminated in this manner; and what a deceptive sense of artistic insight, and comprehensive knowledge, what nescience of the profundity of true spiritual values, is thus engendered. And if we put against this the organic development towards mature spirituality which can only ensue from a constant personal striving for education and intrinsic progress, we shall become aware of the fatal impoverishment that must result from such a *price-reduction* in spiritual goods. The cataracts of music pouring forth from radio stations and other sources day in and day out; the assimilation of musical and literary works to what is supposed to be the taste of the age; the inundation of the masses with entertainments, amusements, diversion, distractions—all this endangers the serious inner life today and spiritual aspirations of those who are exposed to it.

'Civilization'—literally 'the making of citizens'—started off by overcoming sub-civic primitivity in practical life, social attitudes, and educational standards. And certainly, its efforts even in this latter sphere were creditable, as long as, proceeding from an idealistic viewpoint, it instigated the propagation of knowledge and the love of the arts and sciences. These coadjuvant endeavours towards the dissemination of cultural values signified, as it were, an amortization of loans from the gold reserves of culture. In its administration and distribution of cultural values, civilization has proved a true boon to the people; it has brought to large sections of the community not only economic and social betterment, but also a comprehensive improvement in their educational standards.

The present deep-rooted change in the temper of the times, however, can only be explained as due to the ascendancy gained by the materialistic and utilitarian tendencies inherent in modern civilization over those earlier idealistic impulses. Civilization no longer tends to serve a culture which fosters the sciences for the sake of knowledge and which sees in art a manifestation of the higher nature of man and a source of spiritual elevation. The aims of this materialistic civilization are practical progress and utility, prosperity and comfort, and these it sets out to provide for the masses. But in the realm of art, individuality reigns supreme. Culture, in the last resort, stems from and lives in the achievements of eminent individuals: it is the perceptions of the thinker or researcher, the works of the creative artist, the social activities of the philanthropist, the exemplary life and the teachings of the religious man—in short, the supreme achievements of great human personalities—that have created and fecundated culture, and pointed the way to the spiritual development of mankind. The phenomenon, then, to which I have referred, consists in the exploitation of a considerable portion of cultural achievements for purposes of general entertainment. The above-mentioned 'loans from the gold reserves of culture' made in the interest of general education, have become a plundering foray in aid of the mass-consumption of entertainment. In other words: civilization has usurped the administration of cultural values; even worse, it has arrogated to itself the very place of culture itself. In its realm, technology has the function held in the realm of culture by art; not the soul but the intellect is enthroned here. Thus the climate of our world becomes colder; with the increasing perfection of the external conditions of life goes the impoverishment of its intrinsic conditions; cordiality becomes politeness, the desire for education a craving for sensationalism; conversation gives way to television; books to newspapers or illustrated journals; music-making to radio-listening; travelling to sport; and many similar conquests of civilization are at the disposal of the masses as pastimes. Culture, however, does not aim at passing the time; it uses time diligently in the quest for its high purposes; thus it is that we see modern civilization in the role not of a servant to culture but of its opponent, an opponent made dangerous by the fact that it is found in the latter's own camp. For, after all, civilization does belong to the domain of culture, and it is separated from it by no clearly-defined border-line; it can therefore take the arms for its rebellion from the arsenal of its noble sister. The social progress which we owe to civilization is counterbalanced by the cultural regress which its conquering march has produced.

My realization of this fateful turn in cultural development and my concern with its far-reaching consequences has, however, never caused me to avert myself from the present and its impact, or seek refuge in the past. Quite on the contrary: I have attempted to understand what is happening in my time, not merely for the sake of understanding, but because I feel touched by these events as by the hand of fate and wish to shoulder actively the responsibilities that are incurred by this understanding. My immediate task, then, has been to obey the demands of the contemporary spirit in my proper province, that of music. The fact that in this endeavour I have had not only to disappoint the expectations of others, but also to leave my own intentions unfulfilled, has caused me to examine my conscience again and again—with unvarying result, however. Here is the place to speak of this painful experience and to adduce the inner causes that have necessitated my conduct.

A trait of my character which has decisively influenced me from my childhood to this day is the desire to turn to the new and unknown, to widen my horizon. This yearning for approaching and crossing frontiers brought me musical experiences which moved me passionately early on: I remember with clarity the fascination exercised over me when a boy by the bold, revolutionary idiom of Hector Berlioz. The kettle-drum episode at the end of the 'Scene in the Fields', the pungency of the 'March to the Scaffold', and the grotesque savagery of the 'Witches' Sabbath' in the *Symphonie Fantastique*—all these adventurous deviations from the trodden path were felt by me as so many conquering expeditions into the *terra incognita* of music, which irresistibly attracted me. I welcomed the original style of Claude Debussy, and the first performance in Vienna of Schönberg's sextet, *Verklärte Nacht*, which was indignantly rejected by the public, moved me to immediate intense admiration. The radical subjectivity of Mahler's symphonic work and the often extremely daring harmony and polyphony of Richard Strauss—as for instance in the Klytemnestra scenes of *Elektra*—at once became artistic experiences most welcome to me; indeed, it was the episodes of especial audacity in masterpieces such as the 'Funeral March in the manner of Callot' in Mahler's first symphony, or, to name an example of the highest order, the war-music in the Agnus Dei of Beethoven's *Missa Solemnis*, which filled my heart with a sort of intensely personal satisfaction that was over and above my admiration for their greatness. Wherever, to speak with Mephisto, 'a path to the untraversed, untraversable' opened, I was always captivated and intent on elucidation, my interest strongly aroused.

If, in spite of this tendency in my nature, my readiness to perform contemporary works steadily decreased in the course of the years, my conduct was not determined by indolent adhesion to the familiar or truculent rejection of the unfamiliar; for I should have desired nothing more than to be able to fall into step with the spirit of the age. But although the concepts of contemporariness, novelty, and unfamiliarity, and that of the path into the unknown, were highly attractive to me, they could never by themselves become indicators of value for me, and it would be sheer self-negation if, oblivious of the artistic judgment residing within me and fostered by the highest and boldest masterpieces, I took to my heart whatever the day brought, for no better reason than that it was contemporary or novel, unfamiliar or audacious. I rank my responsibility towards the art to which my life is dedicated higher than my duty towards the present, and it would have been wrong for me to make myself the advocate of tendencies which, I am convinced, are leading to its corruption: I am referring here mainly to atonality and dodecaphony which, I fear, are threatening to cause the decay of music. Their overruling importance in present-day musical life enjoins on me the duty of making my position clear, not merely by the omission of such music in my programmes, but also by writing down my views.

The concept of 'tonal music' I consider a pleonasm, for music is by its nature tonal—all our Western music is based on tonality. It is truethat an atonal composition may, by atmospheric qualities or its emotional content, make an impression on people of an artistic cast of mind, intermittently, but it would only be on those who are not really musical. True musicality will not be persuaded by any expressive elements to experience and acknowledge as music an idiom which has been conceived by experimental licence against the autonomous laws of our art and the inner logic of its temporal consecution. In contrast to atonal writing we have dodecaphony, hedged in by strict laws and the product of an abstract system which replaces the elemental logic of our musical progressions by artificial rules. For music, as I have mentioned before, the inherent laws of its progressions are what the rules of grammar are for language; and it is as little possible to speak or write ungrammatically without becoming unintelligible or sinning against language, as it is to accept or understand as music that which violates the most important autonomous laws of musical creation. Atonality and dodecaphony have one—negative—characteristic in common: both reject or deny the laws of modulation immanent in music; their positive relationship is manifested by their abstractness—what they produce is, in a deep sense, divorced from life.

Yet in spite of the abstractness and sterility of this musical Esperanto, musicians of mental vitality have made it their idiom and have succeeded, by the very intensity of their unusual general talents, in developing a considerable dialectical persuasiveness in their works. Since they are lacking in fundamental musicality they have created for themselves an artistic domain of which they believe—with a confidence that is based on their varied musical knowledge, professional skill, and constructive talent, and that remains untroubled by the grace of inspiration which is denied to them—that it represents an entirely novel, *contemporary* epoch of musical creativeness. The living, creative processes of art are replaced by the introduction of abstract working principles, the artificial is substituted for the artistic. Thus, the pronounced trend of our age away from the soul towards the intellect, finds expression in music as well.

The *thematic idea*, this child of truly creative musicianship, is a live birth and has individual qualities; and in his treatment, shaping, and development of it its progenitor should have regard for the child's nature, and not proceed in an arbitrary fashion. The true composer does not behave like a tyrant towards his thematic substance; but he watches like a provident father for signs suggestive of individual development, and lets his creative phantasy be fertilized and directed by these. Such an approach—one of the hall-marks of truly musical creativeness—is fundamentally different from the systematically constructivist method of the dodecaphonists and the arbitrary creative act of the atonal composer. Like Faust's amanuensis, Wagner, these latter declare: 'of the old, senseless mode of procreation we're now well ridden',[1] and instead of a live musical child they bring a homunculus, an artefact, into the world, which, owing to their often astonishing technique of construction, may in fact appear to be an entirely novel artistic product.

In the work of these innovators we must undoubtedly recognize an important, symptomatic phenomenon in the cultural life of our age. For me, it was a bewildering experience; for I found that certain composers of truly creative talent, whose early works had delighted me and with whose music, even in its boldest manifestations, I felt in personal accord, had been capable of making the fateful turn from the artistic to the artificial, from music to non-music; capable, that is, of reconciling the irreconcilable. Under the strong impact made on me by the effective employment by these composers of this non-music

---

[1] Goethe's *Faust*, Part II, Act II, Scene 2: '. . . erklären sie, wie sonst das Zeugen Mode war, für eitel Possen'.

in the service of emotionally genuine dramatism and lyricism I felt compelled again and again to ponder whether it was not, after all, some sort of artistic narrow-mindedness which prevented me from understanding the radical change in the act of musical creation. Yet no, I was not narrow-minded, but I loved music and could not bear to witness its abuse, still less abet it.

The turn from natural to artificial creativeness taken by these composers surely finds its explanation in their, perhaps unconscious, urge to resuscitate their prematurely exhausted creative resources by the tapping of other internal forces—forces, to be sure, that are no longer controlled by the flagging soul, but by the highly alert intellect. On this path they will easily be followed by fellow musicians to whom fate has denied true creative resources; there has thus come into existence that generation of musicians whose works have patently originated in the domain of a strong and acute intellectuality. The latter manifests itself not only in their works but also in their aesthetic ideas, and I cannot but admire the unswerving certainty and determination, and the professional standards of their works, and also the acuity of their frequently highly interesting theoretical dissertations—it is just these merits, however, which show up all too clearly the role taken by the intellect in their mental economy. And I refuse to believe that the mental economy of an artistic personality should be ruled by the intellect. Interesting as the vistas may be that are illumined by its cool, clear light, no true musical life and creativeness will flourish and carol and bear fruit there unless it be fostered by the warming springs rising from deeper layers of the human soul. The intellect does not carol, it does not flourish and bring fruit. Since, therefore, it has no authority in the realm of art, I for my part must refrain from replying to the theories and eloquent dialectics of the atonalists and dodecaphonists with counter-arguments from the same domain, that of the intellect.

What speaks in favour of the representatives of that movement—apart from the impression they give of being able to do what they want—is their courage and uncompromising fighting-spirit; in fact, their moral qualities. On the other hand, the cultural results of these qualities remind me of the stage-action at the end of the second act of Wagner's *Parsifal*: 'The garden withers to a wilderness'.

But even the wilderness, it seems, holds an attraction; it even finds its admirers, though these are of a different kind from those who have enchantedly partaken of the garden's exalted beauty. There are those who seriously wish to investigate the wilderness since they feel the urge to come to terms with the products of a particular *artistic climate* of the present day; there are those whose general spiritual interests are catholic, those who crave for sensation, and those who delight in experiment; but in addition to these, the new extremism in music, as in the other arts, has produced a new type: the Philistine of modern art. In former times, a Philistine was someone who accepted only the familiar in art and rejected anything new. However, the art-snob who accepts everything new just because it is modern and summarily refuses to bother about the art of previous epochs, seems to me the same sort of Philistine. From this type, modern art has recruited a considerable number of followers, and even its wildest departures and excrescences find the approval of these irresolute and indiscriminating minds. They constitute a danger to cultural life since they meet whatever is offered to them not with open, willing souls, but with stolid submission to a catch-word—modernity—whether their bias is positive or negative.

I do not consider it my task here to give a comprehensive survey of the musical present. To describe the variety of present-day musical trends would be a task for the musicologist. My aim was to indicate some of the prominent characteristic features of modern music and show the effect they had on my life, in order to gain a better understanding of the cultural change in the present epoch; and to investigate why I was unable in my activity as a conductor to give expression to my feeling of responsibility towards, and my profound interest in, the present. Now it is certain that the present exerts legitimate power and that we must recognize as obligatory the demands which it makes upon us. But though everything that happens in it has in a certain sense a lasting and permanent effect, the present itself is transient—it is as transient as it is powerful. Does this not offer new hope, and does this thought not exhort us to be ever mindful of the unchanging demands of yet higher powers? It was with this thought in mind that, in spite of my attempts to do justice to the present, I always endeavoured to lift my eyes up above the distressing contemporary scene towards the regions whence come to us those timeless sources of strength. Without deceiving myself about the world-wide crisis of mankind which today endangers our spirit, if not life itself, and whose infiltration into the realm of the arts becomes visible in the signs of their decadence, I was able to maintain a deep confidence and watchful readiness. Though the muses seem exhausted today; though a cold autumn of the soul has called a temporary halt to flowering and fruit-bearing; though the talents and efforts of the present generation are essentially directed to the material and technical; though the spiritual climate of our epoch has perilously changed just as the terrestrial has; my confidence tells me that the genius of mankind shall survive this period of illness once it has remobilized the spiritual and moral powers that are nourished by those lofty springs. 'Where there is danger, the saving forces increase'[1]— with these words of the poet and seer, Friedrich Hölderlin, from his mighty poem *Patmos,* and with the avowal of my ardent faith in his solemn promise shall this dissonant chapter be harmoniously closed.

•

[1] Friedrich Hölderlin (1770 - 1843), *Patmos* (1803): "Wo aber Gefahr ist, wächst das Rettende auch".

Epilogue

At an advanced age, destiny granted me the experience of being introduced to the world of anthroposophy, and I have been able, during recent years, to engross myself in the teachings of Rudolf Steiner. Here, those 'saving forces' of Hölderlin are indeed active; their blessing has descended on me, too, and thus, this book may fittingly close with a tribute to anthroposophy. There is no part of my spiritual self to which the sublime teachings of Rudolf Steiner have not vouchsafed new light and definite advancement. But it is as a musician that I must speak here, lest I overstep the boundaries of my subject. As a musician, I was at first amazed, and later deeply gratified to learn that, in the light that is shed on music by anthroposophy, the dark striving of my young days and my subsequent conscious search for knowledge had indeed put me on the right path, and that my thoughts on the origin and nature of music, the thoughts of a musician though they were, can hold their own in the face of anthroposophy. More than that: in the sublime cosmology of Rudolf Steiner, these thoughts find an incomparably deeper and wiser confirmation; my more intuitive insights are given certainty by being placed in a universal context such as my musicianship by itself could never have provided. Nothing could have shown to me more convincingly my inborn leaning for anthroposophy than my realization that the principal parts of this book, which were written long before my first contact with the teachings of Rudolf Steiner, preserved their essential validity even in the light of my late-gained higher insight. To be sure, the unity of this musical testament of mine was called in question by the onrush of hitherto unsus-

EPILOGUE

pected ideas that inundated my life as I wrote it. However, since the existing part of the book was, as related, in wonderful agreement with Rudolf Steiner's discoveries and remarks about music, I felt encouraged to proceed on the way I had taken; that is, to continue writing as a professional musician, and not as an anthroposophist. What I have written here has not sprung from the soil of anthroposophy, but I am bold enough to believe that, in essentials, the anthroposophist might approve of it. A comprehensive theory of music based on an anthroposophic view of the world lies in the future, and to give it to the world will be the task of some disciples of Rudolf Steiner who are better equipped than I am. This will be nothing less than a fundamentally new method of viewing the history of music as an, as it were, elemental process, and integrating it with the general cultural history of mankind; the systematic application of anthroposophical ideas to the problems of the nature and significance of music will once again demonstrate the range and fruitfulness of these tenets.

I am aware that this task is beyond me—what is needed is a closer, deeper conversancy with Rudolf Steiner's system of teaching than I have been able to acquire in the few years of my studies. But I feel impelled to round off what I have written here as a musician with a tribute to anthroposophy. For—to say it once more—great is my indebtedness to anthroposophy for the immeasurable enrichment it has brought to my old age. It is marvellous to become a student again at my time of life. Throughout my entire being, I feel a rejuvenation which strengthens and invigorates my relation to music, and even my music-making. But this special indebtedness of the musician becomes wholly merged in an overwhelming feeling of all-embracing gratitude that fills my being and demands expression. My changeful, active, music-blessed life has come to rest in this feeling: in gratitude I live, look into the past, look into the future—and look on high.

Beverly Hills,
August 1955.

Index

Compiled by Terence A. Miller, M.S. Ind.

Page numbers in italic indicate musical quotations.
Page numbers in bold type indicate more important references.

215

INDEX

INDEX